2nd EDITION

Pupil Book 5A

T0340587

Series Editor: Peter Clarke

Authors: Elizabeth Jurgensen, Jeanette Mumford, Sandra Roberts

Contents

5-digit numbers

Read and write numbers to 100,000 and determine the value of each digit

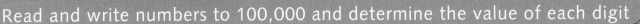

Challenge 1

1 Decompose each of these numbers to show the place value of each digit.

a 6,281   b 3,025   c 8,127   d 5,338

e 7,208   f 3,719   g 8,972   h 6,320

i 2,977   j 6,839   k 9,273   l 9,999

Example

5,284 = 5,000 + 200 + 80 + 4

2 Choose four of the numbers from Question 1 and write them out in words.

Challenge 2

Example

25,872 = 20,000 + 5,000 + 800 + 70 + 2

1 Decompose each of these numbers to show the place value of each digit.

a 16,864   b 27,519   c 46,862   d 53,952

e 75,144   f 83,482   g 91,639   h 78,063

i 61,777   j 83,606   k 76,933   l 99,999

2 Write the numbers that have been partitioned into 10,000s, 1,000s, 100s, 10s and 1s.

a	30,000	4,000	700	80	9
b	50,000	6,000	100	30	2
c	40,000	3,000	800	10	7
d	80,000	1,000	500	70	4
e	10,000	8,000	400	50	3
f	90,000	5,000	200	90	8
g	60,000	2,000	900	60	1
h	50,000	5,000	500	50	5

3 Choose four of the numbers from Question 2 and write them out in words.

1 Write the numbers that have been partitioned into 10,000s, 1,000s, 100s, 10s and 1s.

a	300	40,000	6,000	5	10
b	80	3,000	500	8	20,000
c	7,000	3	40	60,000	300
d	1	700	90	2,000	60,000
e	50	4,000	10,000	3	900
f	800	70,000	1	90	3,000
g	5	900	80,000	50	5,000
h	60,000	5	400	8,000	20

2 Choose four of the numbers from Question 1 and write them out in words.

3 I'm thinking of a number.

- The 10,000s digit is greater than 5.
- The 1,000s digit is smaller than 4.
- The 100s digit is 4.
- The 10s digit is odd.
- The 1s digit is 6.

What could my number be? Write down eight possibilities.

4 Annie is thinking of a number.
What could Annie's number be? Write down five possible answers.

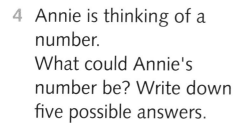

My number is greater than 40,000. It is even. The digits add up to 16, the 1,000s digit is 5 and the 100s digit is less than 3.

Ordering 5-digit numbers

Compare and order numbers to 100,000

Challenge 1

1 Order each set of numbers, smallest to largest.

a 4,871,   2,872,   8,182,   4,927,   3,609,   1,447

b 7,298,   1,724,   3,091,   5,287,   4,327,   1,633

c 5,981,   3,927,   5,719,   3,018,   5,112,   3,904

d 6,911,   7,982,   6,300,   7,275,   6,252,   7,484

e 9,638,   8,027,   9,145,   8,209,   9,222,   8,634

f 2,874,   2,981,   2,071,   2,856,   2,287,   2,251

g 4,823,   4,617,   4,061,   4,187,   4,971,   4,782

h 5,482,   5,439,   5,410,   5,498,   5,428,   5,402

2 Each set of numbers is in order. What could the missing numbers be?

a 2,287,   , 2,867,   , 3,078,   , 3,518

b 4,986,   , 5,100,   , 5,487,   , 5,777

c 5,002,   , 5,265,   , 5,487,   , 5,550

d 5,999,   , 6,010,   , 6,089,   , 6,099

e 6,590,   , 6,620,   , 6,710,   , 6,750

f 7,287,   , 7,376,   , 7,454,   , 7,489

g 8,000,   , 8,100,   , 8,200,   , 8,300

h 9,111,   , 9,222,   , 9,333,   , 9,444

2 1 Order each set of numbers, smallest to largest.

a 23,872, 16,398, 35,982, 26,154, 19,872

b 76,386, 62,612, 59,091, 12,872, 33,886

c 36,989, 30,135, 37,871, 31,832, 30,671

d 45,871, 42,337, 40,871, 48,240, 45,227

e 65,872, 56,397, 65,882, 56,002, 65,255

f 48,655, 84,011, 48,762, 84,330, 48,523

g 79,761, 79,276, 79,023, 79,980, 79,548

h 91,122, 91,101, 91,012, 91,121, 91,001

2 Write any number that lies between each pair of numbers and still keeps the order.

a | 24,871 | 28,901 | b | 30,800 | 31,800 | c | 42,872 | 43,872 |

d | 50,107 | 50,565 | e | 25,982 | 25,997 | f | 45,876 | 45,884 |

g | 71,009 | 71,020 | h | 86,333 | 87,338 | i | 60,576 | 60,582 |

 1 Use the digit cards to make ten different 5-digit numbers.

2 Order your numbers, smallest to largest.

Hint
Organising your numbers in a systematic way will help you to check that you do not repeat any answers.

5-digit counting

Count forwards and backwards in steps of 10 and 100

Challenge 1

1 Count on in 10s from these start numbers.

a 4,316,   ,   , 4,346,   ,   ,

b 5,753,   ,   ,   ,   , 5,803,

c 2,694,   ,   ,   ,   , 2,744,

d 8,067,   ,   , 8,097,   ,   ,

e 6,599,   ,   ,   ,   ,   ,

2 Using the same start numbers as in Question 1, count back eight steps in 10s.

3 Count on in 100s from these start numbers.

a 2,762,   ,   , 3,062,   ,   ,

b 3,276,   ,   ,   , 3,676,   ,

c 5,861,   ,   ,   ,   , 6,361,

d 7,534,   ,   , 7,834,   ,   ,

e 6,725,   ,   ,   ,   ,   ,

4 Using the same start numbers as in Question 3, count back eight steps in 100s.

Challenge 2

1 Count on in 10s from these start numbers.

a 41,763,   ,   ,   , 41,803,   ,

b 28,741,   ,   ,   ,   , 28,791,

c 33,285,   ,   , 33,315,   ,   ,

d 58,531,   ,   ,   ,   ,   , 58,591

e 72,868,   ,   ,   ,   ,   ,

2 Using the same start numbers as in Question 1, count back eight steps in 10s.

3 Count on in 100s from these start numbers.

   a   18,652,   ,   ,   , 19,052,   ,

   b   26,482,   ,   ,   ,   , 26,982,

   c   61,875,   ,   ,   , 62,275,   ,

   d   57,946,   ,   , 58,246,   ,   ,

   e   72,931,   ,   ,   ,   ,   ,

   f   65,428,   ,   ,   ,   ,   ,

4 Using the same start numbers as in Question 3, count back eight steps in 100s.

1 Explain which digits change when counting on and back with 5-digit numbers:

   a   in 10s   b   in 100s

2 Play this game with a partner.

- One player chooses a 5-digit start number.

- In your heads, both count on in 10s five times.

- Write down the number you get to. Do you and your partner have the same number?

- If not, count together out loud to find the right answer.

- Do this ten times, taking turns to choose the start number.

Repeat the steps above, this time counting back in 10s, or on or back in 100s.

54,397, 54,407, 54,417, 54,427, 54,437, 54,447

5-digit rounding

Round numbers up to 100,000 to the nearest 10, 100 and 1,000

1 Write the two multiples of 10 that each number lies between on either side of the number.

Example
2,780 ← 2,784 → 2,790

a 2,763   b 1,951   c 4,287   d 6,159   e 7,395

f 8,218   g 4,832   h 5,624   i 8,916   j 4,893

2 Look at the 1s digit in each number in Question 1 and decide whether the number rounds up or down. Circle the multiple of 10 that the number rounds to.

Example
(2,780) ← 2,784 → 2,790

1 Write the two multiples of 10 that each number lies between on either side of the number. Look at the 1s digit and circle the multiple of 10 that the number rounds to.

a 25,824   b 18,769   c 36,523   d 41,995   e 57,168

f 68,221   g 48,637   h 73,524   i 36,885   j 83,482

2 Using the numbers in Question 1, write the two multiples of 100 that each number lies between on either side of the number. Look at the 10s digit and circle the multiple of 100 that the number rounds to.

Example
(26,700) ← 26,716 → 26,800

3 Using the numbers in Question 1, write the two multiples of 1,000 that each number lies between on either side of the number. Look at the 100s digit and circle the multiple of 1,000 that the number rounds to.

4 What number is Rosie describing? Write down ten possible answers.

If I round my number to the nearest 100 it is 46,800. If I round it to the nearest 1,000 it is 47,000.

5 What number is Daniel describing?

My number is between 75,000 and 80,000. It is a multiple of 5. No digit in my number is less than 3 or greater than 7. The 1,000s digit is 1 more than the 1s digit. The 100s digit is larger than the 10s digit.

Challenge 3

1 Explain clearly the rules for rounding numbers.
   You could make them into a poster for your class to refer to.

2 Solve these problems.

a The cost of decorating a school was estimated at £37,585. What is this figure to the nearest £100?

b A company made a profit of £93,865 in one year. What is this figure to the nearest £10?

c A newspaper sold 65,277 copies. What is this figure to the nearest 1,000?

d A total of 34,631 people registered to run in a marathon. Round this number to the nearest 10, 100 and 1,000. Which figure do you think the organisers rounded it to when ordering the water bottles needed? Explain your answer.

e Two companies rounded their profits to the nearest £1,000 and both figures were £45,000. The first manager said 'My company made £900 more than the second company!' What could the two profits have been? Give three possible answers.

f A town has a population of 84,136. What is this number rounded to the nearest 10, 100 and 1,000? Think of a time when the town council may use a rounded number instead of an exact number. Which figure would they use and why?

Adding mentally (1)

Add numbers mentally

Challenge 1

1 Add these numbers mentally.

a 1,582 + 50   b 1,491 + 80

c 2,743 + 60   d 2,855 + 70

e 2,963 + 90   f 2,561 + 30

g 3,127 + 50   h 3,483 + 40

i 4,175 + 60   j 5,864 + 80

2 Add these numbers mentally.

a 1,473 + 360   b 1,362 + 470

c 2,591 + 390   d 2,468 + 620

e 2,954 + 540   f 3,729 + 250

g 4,276 + 630   h 5,187 + 810

i 6,455 + 720   j 7,452 + 950

2,997 + 60 =

997 + 60 = 1,057

2,997 + 60 = 3,057

Challenge 2

1 Add these numbers mentally.

a 13,544 + 70   b 24,561 + 50   c 29,782 + 40

d 36,981 + 60   e 42,593 + 70   f 51,651 + 90

g 54,783 + 80   h 60,871 + 50   i 64,263 + 90

2 Add these numbers mentally.

a 17,456 + 500   b 23,163 + 700   c 38,439 + 400

d 45,612 + 600   e 56,288 + 900   f 60,756 + 800

g 61,763 + 400   h 65,825 + 700   i 71,503 + 900

3 Add these numbers mentally.

   a   16,871 + 3,000   b   25,871 + 5,000   c   31,287 + 6,000

   d   44,287 + 9,000   e   53,899 + 8,000   f   65,402 + 7,000

   g   49,873 + 6,000   h   62,871 + 8,000   i   65,692 + 7,000

1 Add these numbers mentally.

   a   37,298 + 60   b   46,198 + 300

   c   50,261 + 80   d   63,498 + 5,000

   e   72,981 + 700   f   75,507 + 90

   g   81,762 + 800   h   87,366 + 7,000

   i   90,621 + 900   j   95,289 + 6,000

$$33,647 + 70 =$$
$$647 + 70 = 717$$
$$33,647 + 70 = 33,717$$

2 Add these numbers mentally.

   a   28,567 + 320   b   17,608 + 1,300

   c   32,459 + 510   d   44,821 + 630

   e   57,431 + 2,400   f   49,655 + 750

   g   63,278 + 5,080   h   79,326 + 3,700

   i   86,812 + 640   j   89,650 + 2,500

3 Work out the missing numbers.

   a   61,405 + ____ = 62,205   b   47,246 + ____ = 52,246

   c   54,689 + ____ = 54,759   d   32,534 + ____ = 33,254

   e   26,197 + ____ = 31,797   f   ____ + 60 = 79,376

   g   ____ + 4,000 = 22,752   h   ____ + 800 = 54,778

   i   ____ + 550 = 84,911   j   ____ + 2,700 = 38,523

4 Explain how you worked out the calculations in Question 3.

Subtracting mentally (1)

Subtract numbers mentally

 Challenge 1

1 Subtract these numbers mentally.

a   1,762 – 40   b   2,876 – 60   c   3,149 – 50

d   4,751 – 80   e   4,527 – 40   f   5,836 – 70

g   5,802 – 20   h   6,387 – 90   i   7,325 – 30

j   8,658 – 70   k   7,762 – 80   l   8,342 – 50

2 Subtract these numbers mentally.

a   1,529 – 210   b   2,387 – 350   c   3,981 – 460

d   3,376 – 420   e   4,898 – 640   f   4,739 – 590

g   5,376 – 450   h   6,815 – 760   i   7,481 – 610

j   8,457 – 740   k   8,145 – 360   l   8,562 – 750

 Challenge 2

1 Subtract these numbers mentally.

a   18,873 – 60   b   26,169 – 80   c   30,615 – 50

d   45,811 – 40   e   51,706 – 60   f   57,541 – 80

g   61,652 – 70   h   63,703 – 40   i   68,652 – 90

2 Subtract these numbers mentally.

a   18,987 – 500   b   29,726 – 800

c   37,655 – 700   d   41,239 – 400

e   55,188 – 600   f   64,387 – 900

g   62,329 – 500   h   65,618 – 700

i   71,063 – 300   j   70,568 – 700

3 Subtract these numbers mentally.

    a   16,752 – 4,000   b 22,871 – 5,000   c 36,874 – 7,000

    d   47,287 – 9,000   e 54,829 – 6,000   f 67,114 – 8,000

    g   51,753 – 4,000   h 67,826 – 8,000   i 70,104 – 7,000

1 Subtract these numbers mentally.

    a   34,761 – 90   b 49,243 – 700   c 52,893 – 5,000

    d   67,298 – 800   e 74,904 – 70   f 70,855 – 900

    g   83,562 – 7,000   h 86,477 – 600   i 93,633 – 60

2 Subtract these numbers mentally.

    a   25,298 – 310   b 39,083 – 3,400   c 47,388 – 5,020

    d   51,942 – 3,500   e 65,133 – 570   f 72,543 – 830

    g   85,627 – 6,400   h 93,225 – 890   i 94,397 – 530

3 Work out the missing numbers.

    a   63,398 – ____ = 63,158   b 42,274 – ____ = 36,174

    c   21,385 – ____ = 15,585   d 79,612 – ____ = 79,572

    e   63,293 – ____ = 58,693   f ____ – 2,700 = 71,379

    g   ____ – 2,300 = 14,491   h ____ – 60 = 38,153

    i   ____ – 8,600 = 82,876   j ____ – 6,800 = 82,704

4 Write ten calculations for your partner to work out. Make sure you can do them mentally first.

Subtracting mentally (2)

Subtract numbers mentally

Challenge 1

1 Work out these calculations. Use either the finding the difference method or rounding and adjusting.

a 3,672 – 399   b 1,276 – 59   c 3,827 – 598

d 5,282 – 499   e 2,321 – 89   f 5,745 – 898

g 6,261 – 999   h 7,629 – 798   i 6,814 – 643

2 Work out these calculations.

a 3,930 – 1,999   b 4,270 – 1,998   c 4,820 – 2,999

d 5,820 – 2,998   e 6,380 – 3,999   f 6,200 – 3,998

g 7,030 – 4,999   h 8,250 – 4,998   i 8,020 – 1,998

Challenge 2

1 Work out these calculations. Use either the finding the difference method or rounding and adjusting.

a 25,200 – 2,999   b 27,360 – 3,998   c 35,280 – 3,999

d 39,400 – 4,998   e 42,560 – 5,999   f 56,380 – 6,998

g 52,542 – 6,999   h 57,287 – 7,998   i 61,273 – 8,999

2 Work out these calculations.

a 18,270 – 12,999   b 24,170 – 15,998   c 27,870 – 19,999

d 36,997 – 21,999   e 46,291 – 18,998   f 48,755 – 25,998

g 56,726 – 26,999   h 58,465 – 31,998   i 62,820 – 45,999

3 Explain which method you prefer to use for the calculations in Questions 1 and 2.

4 Work with a partner.

One of you should use a written method and the other a mental method to work out each of these calculations.

Both write down each calculation and start at the same time.

a 57,398 – 5,999   b 28,428 – 6,001   c 62,593 – 4,998

Compare the answers. Who was the first to work out the correct answer?

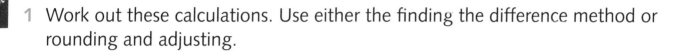

1 Work out these calculations. Use either the finding the difference method or rounding and adjusting.

a 45,786 – 26,999   b 49,276 – 31,998   c 57,798 – 29,999

d 53,299 – 31,998   e 60,897 – 28,999   f 78,045 – 37,998

g 81,801 – 42,997   h 93,400 – 52,995   i 72,444 – 61,995

2 Work out these calculations.

a 49,761 – 12,001   b 52,295 – 15,002   c 63,288 – 25,001

d 68,711 – 30,002   e 73,982 – 41,003   f 82,998 – 52,004

g 87,855 – 58,002   h 99,999 – 60,003   i 94,811 – 21,002

3 Work out the missing numbers.

a 47,623 –   = 11,626   b 79,859 –   = 46,860

c 21,396 –   = 7,393   d 35,368 –   = 18,370

e 17,429 –   = 5,427   f   – 47,001 = 17,386

g   – 63,005 = 34,618   h   – 38,996 = 12,813

i   – 57,002 = 27,150   j   – 28,995 = 8,926

4 Explain how you worked out the calculations in Question 2.

5 Do you think it is useful to be able to calculate mentally with large numbers? Explain your reasons.

Computer game problems

Solve addition and subtraction multi-step problems, deciding which operations and methods to use and why

Class 5A are playing a new computer game.

Challenge 1

1   Jack scored 7,252 on his first game. On his second game, his score increased by 599. What was his new score?

2   Hussain and Shelina are having a race to see who can be the first to hit the top score of 10,000.

   a   Hussain thinks his score of 9,400 makes him likely to win. How many more does he need to score?

   b   Shelina needs another 780. What is her score now?

3   Molly and Jack compare their scores. Molly has 3,500 less than Jack. He has 6,990. What is Molly's score?

4   Shelina was really pleased with her new score of 8,540, but then she lost 799 because of a mistake. What was her new score?

Challenge 2

1   Hussain increased his score on the game from 35,724 to 38,724 on one day. The next day he increased his score by twice as much. What is his new score?

2   Jack's target for the game he is playing is 50,000. His score from each time he plays counts towards his target. The first two times he played he scored 18,999 and 21,600. How far away from his target is he?

3   Hussain was beaten by his friend today. His friend scored 56,302, which was 17,999 better than Hussain. What was Hussain's score?

4   Jack, Molly and Shelina are comparing scores. Their scores are 45,640, 67,640 and 70,001. What is the difference between the highest and lowest scores?

5   In their new game, Molly has scored 2,800 less than Jack. Jack has scored 5,999 less than Shelina. Shelina's score is 28,600. What are Molly's and Jack's scores?

6   Make up a word problem, based on computer games, for a partner. Use the operations + and −.

Challenge 3

1   Molly is always trying to beat her score. Today, Thursday, her best score is 45,780. This is an increase of 12,999 on Wednesday's score, and an increase of 15,000 on Tuesday's score. What did she score on Tuesday and Wednesday?

2   Molly and Jack are having a race to see who can be the first to hit the top score of 100,000. Molly is currently 36,800 ahead of Jack, although Jack's score is higher than 50,000. Molly's score contains 5 different digits. What could their scores be?

3   When Shelina got a score of 25,999, the computer tripled it. Unfortunately, she then lost 21,500 because of a mistake. What is her new score?

4   Hussain's last three scores are 34,500, 38,999 and 25,702. If he totals them up, how many more does he need to hit the jackpot of 100,000?

5   Make up a word problem, based on computer games, for a partner. Use the operations + and − and ×.

Faces and edges in 3-D shapes

Identify 3-D shapes with parallel or perpendicular faces or edges

Challenge 1

This cupboard is a cuboid and is fixed to a wall.

The four vertices of the rectangular face of the cupboard are labelled A, B, C and D.

Copy and complete each sentence using the word 'parallel' or 'perpendicular'.

a   AD is   to BC.

b   DC is   to AB.

c   AD is   to DC.

d   DC is   to CB.

e   DA is   to AB.

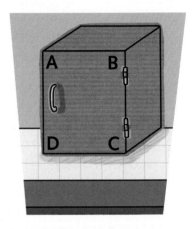

Example
AB is parallel to DC.
AB is perpendicular to BC.

Challenges 2,3

1   Four 3-D shapes are placed on a horizontal shelf.
    Copy and complete the table for the faces of each 3-D shape.

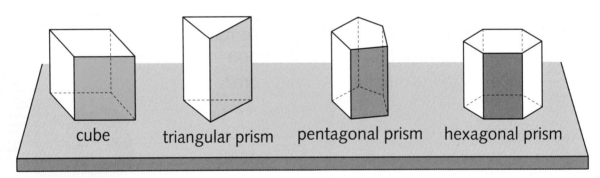

cube   triangular prism   pentagonal prism   hexagonal prism

3-D shape	Total number of faces	Number of faces perpendicular to the shelf	Number of faces parallel to the shelf
cube	6	4	
triangular prism			
pentagonal prism			
hexagonal prism			

2 Copy and complete the table below for the edges of each 3-D shape in Question 1.

3-D shape	Total number of edges	Number of edges perpendicular to the shelf	Number of edges parallel to the shelf
cube	12	4	
triangular prism			
pentagonal prism			
hexagonal prism			

3 These two 3-D shapes are placed on a horizontal shelf. Copy and complete each sentence using the word 'parallel' or 'perpendicular'.

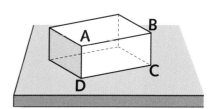

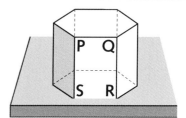

a   AB is _____ to DC.   b   AD is _____ to BC.

c   AD is _____ to DC.   d   PS is _____ to SR.

e   PQ is _____ to QR.   f   QR is _____ to PS.

4 Each of the 3-D shapes below is placed on a shelf and lies on a rectangular face.

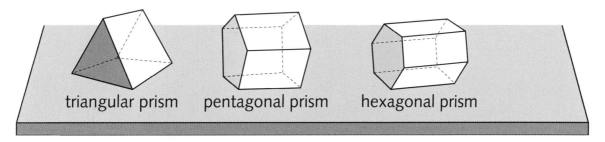

triangular prism   pentagonal prism   hexagonal prism

a   Copy the tables in Questions 1 and 2 but leave out the row for cube. Complete the tables for each shape.

b   Compare your answers with those you completed in Questions 1 and 2. Write what you notice.

:nge

This cube is placed on a horizontal table.

a   How many faces are parallel to the shaded face?

b   How many faces are perpendicular to the shaded face?

c   Name three pairs of parallel edges.

d   Name three pairs of perpendicular edges.

21

Identifying 3-D shapes

Use properties to identify 3-D shapes

Challenge 1

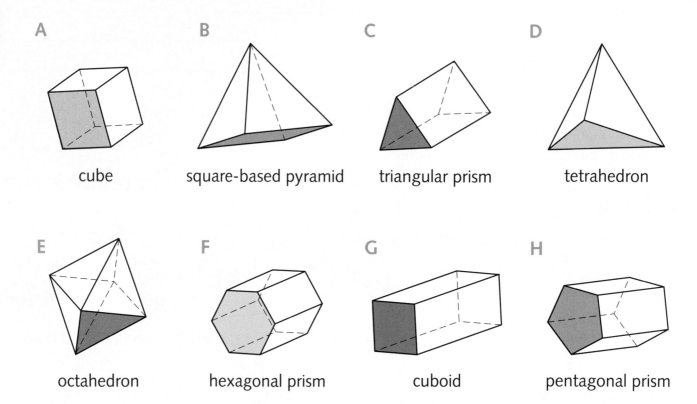

A	B	C	D
cube	square-based pyramid	triangular prism	tetrahedron

E	F	G	H
octahedron	hexagonal prism	cuboid	pentagonal prism

1 Look at the 3-D shapes above. Copy the table and write in the letters of the shapes.

No faces with four right angles	
Only one face with four right angles	
More than one face with four right angles	
Three edges at each vertex	
More than three edges at one or more vertices	

2 Write the name of the 3-D shape that:

a is a prism with six rectangular faces

b has four edges meeting at every vertex and all faces triangular.

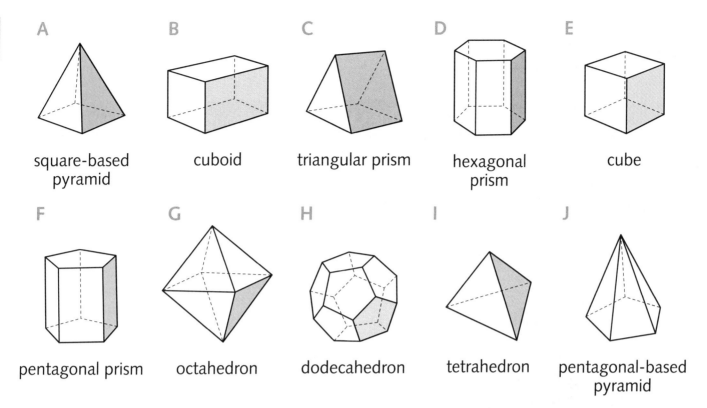

A square-based pyramid

B cuboid

C triangular prism

D hexagonal prism

E cube

F pentagonal prism

G octahedron

H dodecahedron

I tetrahedron

J pentagonal-based pyramid

1   Look at the 3-D shapes above. Copy the table and write in the letters of the shapes.

	Three edges at each vertex	More than three edges at one or more vertices
No right-angled faces		
One right-angled face		
More than one right-angled face		

2   Write the name of the 3-D shape that has:

a   eight vertices and all right-angled faces are identical

b   one face which is not right-angled and five edges meeting at one of the vertices

c   four more vertices than a cube with two identical and regular end faces

d   all faces regular but neither triangular nor right-angled.

Look at the 3-D shapes in Challenge 2. Name the 3-D shapes that have the properties of a regular polyhedron.

Rule
In a regular polyhedron:
• each face is a regular polygon
• all faces are identical
• the same number of faces meet at each vertex.

Drawing 3-D shapes

Visualise and draw 3-D shapes from the top, from the front and from the side

Challenge 1

You can view 3-D shapes in three ways:
from the top, from the front and from the side.

You will need:
- 20 centicubes in five colours: red, blue, green, yellow and orange
- five coloured pencils
- 1 cm square dot paper
- ruler

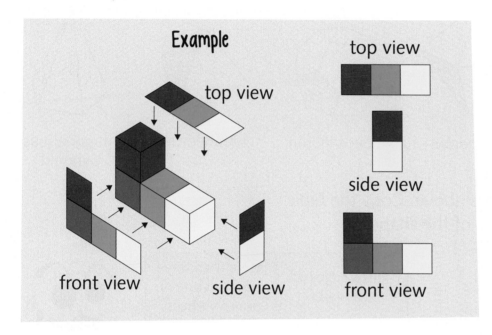

1 Make the 3-D shape on the right with four centicubes.
Draw it on square dot paper as you would see it from the

a   top view   b   front view   c   side view.

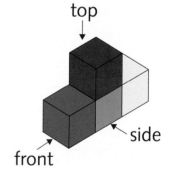

2 Use the three views to make each shape with centicubes.

a   top view   front view   side view

b   top view   front view   side view

1 Look at the diagrams below.

a Make each 3-D shape with centicubes.

b Draw it on square dot paper as you would see it from the top, the front and the side.

You will need:
- 20 centicubes in six colours: red, blue, green, yellow, orange and purple
- six coloured pencils
- 1 cm square dot paper
- ruler

A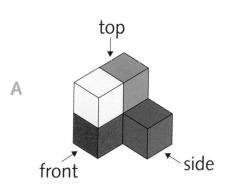

B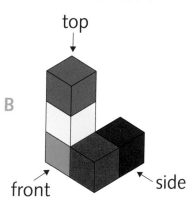

C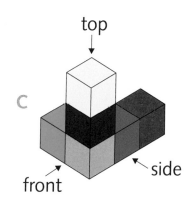

2 Use the three views to make each shape with centicubes.

a   top view   front view   side view

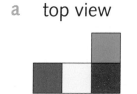

b   top view   front view   side view

 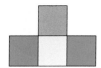

c   top view   front view   side view

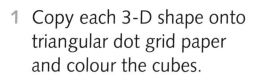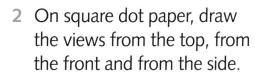

1 Copy each 3-D shape onto triangular dot grid paper and colour the cubes.

2 On square dot paper, draw the views from the top, from the front and from the side.

A    B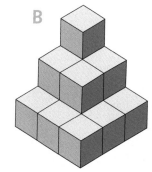

You will need:
- coloured pencil
- 1 cm triangular dot grid paper
- 1 cm square dot paper
- ruler

Working with 3-D shapes

Investigate and draw 3-D shapes which can be made using interlocking cubes

This drawing shows the six cubes which make the 3-D shape.

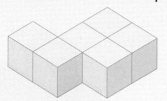

This is a drawing of the same 3-D shape but it does not show the individual cubes.

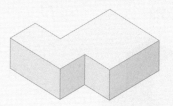

Challenge 1

1 For each shape below:

- estimate the least number of cubes you will need to build each shape
- build the shape
- write the number of cubes you needed.

You will need:
- 12 centicubes

A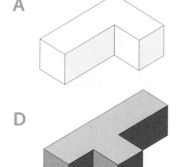

B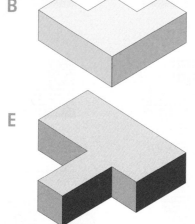

C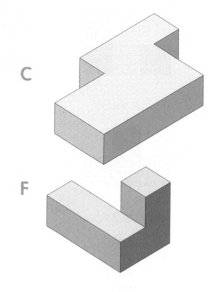

D

E

F

2 Carla used five cubes to build her shape. She decorated her shape with star stickers. Write the letter of the shape that is exactly the same as Carla's.

Carla's shape:

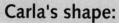
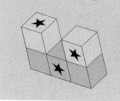

A 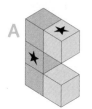 B 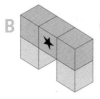 C 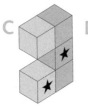 D 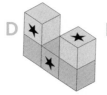 E  F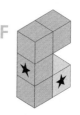

1 Follow the instructions in Challenge 1, Question 1 for these shapes.

You will need:
- 12 centicubes

A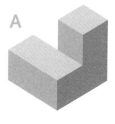

B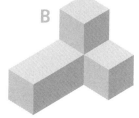

C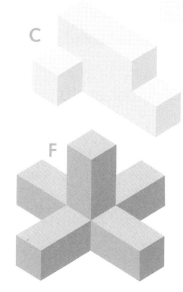

D

E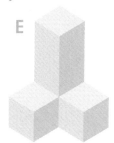

F

2 Each of the 3-D shapes below is made with six cubes. Which drawings show the same shape but have different orientations and colours?

Hint
One shape does not have a match.

A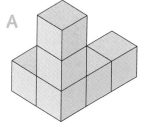

B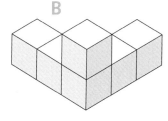

C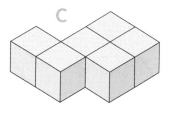

D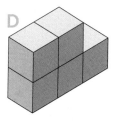

E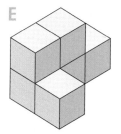

F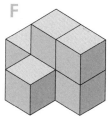

G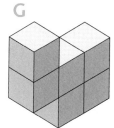

H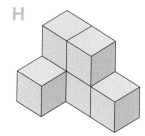

I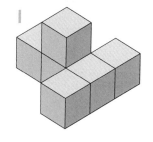

Build three different shapes with six cubes. Draw each shape you make on triangular dot paper.

You will need:
- 18 centicubes
- 1 cm triangular dot paper
- ruler

Multiplying by 9, 99 using 10, 100 and adjusting

Multiply numbers mentally using known facts

Challenge 1

1 Multiply each number by 10.

a 23   b 47   c 72   d 58   e 84

Example
43 × 10 = 430

2 Multiply each number by 100.

a 39   b 77   c 28   d 85   e 46

Example
43 × 100 = 4,300

Challenge 2

1 Multiply each number by 9. Multiply by 10 first, then adjust to find the answer.

Example
43 × 9 = (43 × 10) − 43
= 430 − 43
= 387

a 67   b 89   c 69   d 37   e 63

f 34   g 45   h 58   i 74   j 92

2 Multiply each number by 99. Multiply by 100 first, then adjust to find the answer.

Example
43 × 99 = (43 × 100) − 43
= 4,300 − 43
= 4,257

a 46   b 37   c 25   d 74   e 93

f 83   g 58   h 62   i 41   j 86

3 Use a calculator to work out the answers to these calculations. What patterns do you notice?

Predict what the next answer in the pattern will be.

You will need:
• calculator

9 × 9		9 × 99		9 × 999

Challenge 3

1 Work out the calculations below. Two slightly different strategies are required. Sort the calculations into two sets, one set for each strategy.

Explain your reasoning.

a 45 × 9   b 84 × 9   c 63 × 9

d 72 × 9   e 56 × 9   f 78 × 9

g 67 × 9   h 75 × 9   i 26 × 9

j 37 × 9   k 68 × 9   l 53 × 9

2 Use a mental strategy to work out the answers to these calculations.

a 35 × 199   b 33 × 299   c 54 × 198

d 26 × 198   e 15 × 396   f 22 × 397

g 18 × 298   h 32 × 499   i 41 × 297

j 43 × 298   k 64 × 399   l 81 × 598

3 Use a calculator to work out the answers to these calculations. What patterns do you notice?

Predict what the next answer in the pattern will be when your calculator display is not big enough.

You will need:
• calculator

99 × 99		999 × 999		9,999 × 9,999

Multiplying by multiples of 10, 100 and 1,000

Multiply whole numbers by multiples of 10, 100 and 1,000

 Challenge 1

1 a 10 × 36   2 a 10 × 48   3 a 74 × 10   4 a 10 × 27

 b 100 × 36   b 100 × 48   b 74 × 100   b 100 × 27

 c 1,000 × 36   c 1,000 × 48   c 74 × 1,000   c 1,000 × 27

5 a 10 × 53   6 a 65 × 10   7 a 10 × 81

 b 100 × 53   b 65 × 100   b 100 × 81

 c 1,000 × 53   c 65 × 1,000   c 1,000 × 81

Challenge 2

1 Work out the answer to each calculation.

 a 24 × 3   b 37 × 2   c 58 × 4   d 36 × 8   e 45 × 7   f 64 × 4

2 These calculations are related to the calculations in Question 1. Find the related facts and work out the answers by using your knowledge of multiples of 10, 100 and 1,000.

58 × 40   36 × 8,000   37 × 200   45 × 7,000   24 × 30

45 × 700   64 × 400   24 × 300   58 × 400   36 × 800

64 × 40   58 × 4,000   45 × 70   36 × 80   37 × 2,000

3 Use these calculations to write your own related facts involving multiples of 10, 100 and 1,000.

a 28 × 9   b 57 × 8   c 73 × 7   d 68 × 6   e 86 × 5   f 63 × 4

4 How many 2-digit numbers can you find that are 10 times as big as the 2 digits added together? What are the numbers?

1 Write the missing multiple of 10, 100 or 1,000.

10

100

1,000

a 45 ×  = 1,350   b 63 × 30 =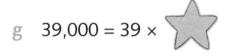

c 26 × = 780   d 64 × = 12,800

e 37 × = 1,480   f 46 × = 27,600

g 39,000 = 39 ×   h 35 × 40 =

i 48 × = 240,000   j 186,000 = 62 ×

k 43,200 = 54 ×   l 57 × 600 =

m 76,000 = 19 ×   n 30 × = 5,100

2 Write the number that matches each clue.

a I am 10 times larger than 456 ÷ 4 added to 324 ÷ 6.

b I am 1,000 times smaller than double 7,500.

c I am the same as 400 multiplied by 27 added to 300 multiplied by 84.

Multiplying using multiples of 10 and adjusting

Multiply numbers mentally using known facts

Challenge 1

1   Multiply each number by 10.

Example
36 × 10 = 360

a 53   b 27   c 82   d 65   e 48

f 36   g 74   h 91   i 18   j 60

2   Multiply these numbers.

Example
43 × 4 = (43 × 2) + (43 × 2)
= 86 + 86
= 172

a 27 × 9   b 7 × 65   c 53 × 5

d 82 × 8   e 6 × 48   f 36 × 4

g 73 × 8   h 95 × 6   i 7 × 74

Challenge 2

1   Multiply each number by 19. Multiply by a multiple of 10 first, then adjust to find the answer.

Example
23 × 19 = (23 × 20) − 23
= 460 − 23
= 437

a 24   b 45   c 36   d 48

e 64   f 56   g 77   h 85

2 Multiply each number by 29. Multiply by a multiple
  of 10 first, then adjust to find the answer.

a 23   b 15   c 37   d  44   e 63

3 Multiply each number by 39. Multiply by a multiple
  of 10 first, then adjust to find the answer.

a  16   b 27   c 45   d 53

e 62   f 41   g 80   h 74

4 Work out the answers to these calculations by multiplying
  by a multiple of 10 first, then adjusting to find the answer.

a  38 × 49   b  35 × 69   c  26 × 79   d  24 × 59

e 47 × 59   f 29 × 34   g  49 × 55   h 19 × 84

Mary tried to use the multiplying by multiples of 10 and
then adjusting strategy to work out these answers quickly.
For which calculations would this be a good strategy?

a  44 × 28   b  36 × 41   c  43 × 56

d  32 × 21   e  56 × 64   f  29 × 15

g  61 × 16   h  38 × 24   i  59 × 67

Multiplying and halving

- Multiply and divide numbers mentally using known facts
- Multiply and divide whole numbers by 10 and 100

Challenge 1

1 Halve each number mentally.

	i		ii		iii		iv		v	
a	i	480	ii	260	iii	840	iv	420	v	640
b	i	560	ii	380	iii	140	iv	720	v	940
c	i	150	ii	370	iii	530	iv	390	v	750

2 Which set of numbers was the easiest to halve? Explain why.

Challenges 2, 3

1 Multiply each number by 5 mentally. First multiply by 10, then divide by 2.

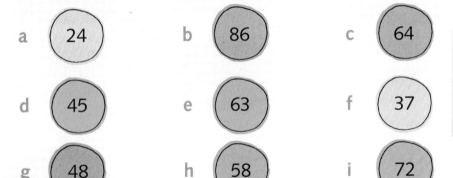

Example
$28 \times 5 = (28 \times 10) \div 2$
$= 280 \div 2$
$= 140$

2 Multiply each number by 50 mentally. First multiply by 100, then divide by 2.

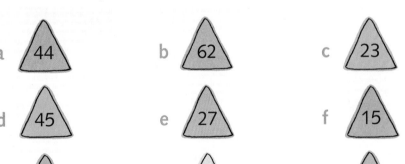

Example
$28 \times 50 = (28 \times 100) \div 2$
$= 2,800 \div 2$
$= 1,400$

3 Multiply each number by 25 mentally. First multiply by 100, then divide by 2 and divide by 2 again.

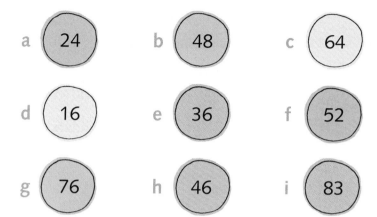

a 24   b 48   c 64

d 16   e 36   f 52

g 76   h 46   i 83

Example
$28 \times 25 = (28 \times 100) \div 2 \div 2$
$= 2{,}800 \div 2 \div 2$
$= 1{,}400 \div 2$
$= 700$

4 Work out the answers to these calculations mentally using the most appropriate strategy.

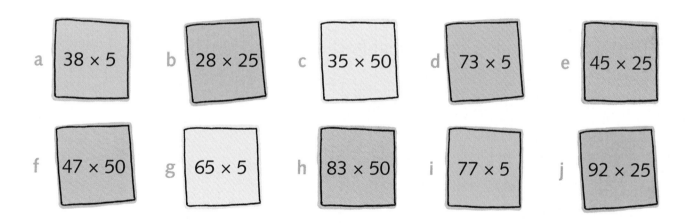

a 38 × 5   b 28 × 25   c 35 × 50   d 73 × 5   e 45 × 25

f 47 × 50   g 65 × 5   h 83 × 50   i 77 × 5   j 92 × 25

1 Look carefully at the mental calculations you completed in Challenges 2, 3. Some calculations are much easier to work out mentally than others. Can you find an easy and a more difficult calculation for × 5, × 50 and × 25 and explain why some are easier than others?

2 Work out the missing numbers.

a $67 \times \boxed{} = 1{,}675$ b $\boxed{} \times 5 = 170$ c $86 \times \boxed{} = 4{,}300$

d $\boxed{} \times 50 = 3{,}850$ e $93 \times \boxed{} = 465$ f $\boxed{} \times 25 = 1{,}450$

Finding fractions

Find fractions of numbers and quantities using fractions as operators

1 Work out these unit fractions.

a $\frac{1}{2}$ of 48   b $\frac{1}{5}$ of 110

c $\frac{1}{3}$ of 51   d $\frac{1}{6}$ of 84

e $\frac{1}{3}$ of 72   f $\frac{1}{6}$ of 108

g $\frac{1}{5}$ of 70   h $\frac{1}{7}$ of 126

Remember, a unit fraction is a fraction with 1 as the numerator. $\frac{1}{3}$ is a unit fraction.

Example

$\frac{1}{3}$ of 36 = 36 ÷ 3

= 12

2 In each of the models below, what fraction of each cake is left?

1 All of these mugs can hold 300 ml of coffee.

a What fraction of the coffee is left in each mug?

b How much coffee is left in each mug? Write your answer in mililitres.

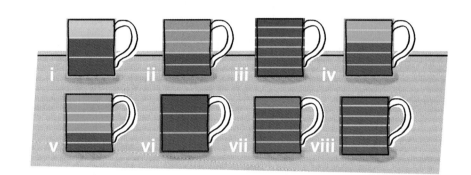

2 Work out these non-unit fractions.

a $\frac{2}{3}$ of £72

b $\frac{3}{5}$ of 145 km

c $\frac{2}{6}$ of 114 g

d $\frac{4}{5}$ of 170

e $\frac{2}{3}$ of 102 hours

f $\frac{4}{7}$ of £147

g $\frac{5}{6}$ of 168 kg

h $\frac{3}{8}$ of 192 km

Example

$\frac{3}{4}$ of £108 = (£108 ÷ 4) × 3

= £27 × 3

= £81

1 Explain how to work out non-unit fractions. You could write this out as a set of instructions for your class to use.

2 Two friends are travelling the same journey of 312 km. One has travelled $\frac{6}{8}$ of the distance and the other has travelled $\frac{4}{6}$ of the journey. Who has travelled further?

3 Which of these two fractions is closest to a whole? How can you prove this?

4 A farmer has 450 acres of land.

a He is going to divide it up and sell it as plots of land all the same size. Write five different possible ways he could do this, as fractions. For example, $\frac{1}{2} + \frac{1}{2}$.

b If the whole land is worth £11,250, how much should he sell each of the plots of land for in each of your examples? For example, £5,625 per plot if he divided it into 2 equal plots.

Fraction sequences

- Count forwards and backwards in simple fractions
- Recognise fraction sequences and find the term-to-term rule

Challenge 1

1 Hamish is counting in fractions.
   - Continue the count in halves.
   - Write the fractions as you say them.
   - Stop when you get to 10.

$\frac{1}{2}$, 1, $1\frac{1}{2}$, 2, $2\frac{1}{2}$, 3, ...

2 Vicky is counting in fractions.
   - Continue the count in quarters.
   - Write the fractions as you say them.
   - Stop when you get to 5.

$\frac{1}{4}$, $\frac{2}{4}$, $\frac{3}{4}$, 1, $1\frac{1}{4}$, $1\frac{2}{4}$, ...

3 Sally is counting in fractions.
   - Continue the count in thirds.
   - Write the fractions as you say them.
   - Stop when you get to 7.

$\frac{1}{3}$, $\frac{2}{3}$, 1, $1\frac{1}{3}$, $1\frac{2}{3}$, 2, ...

Challenge 2

1 For each question, follow the steps below.
   - Write the start number shown in the table on the right.
   - Count on in the fraction listed up to the end number.
   - Record the fractions as you count.

	Start	Fraction	End
a	8	halves	15
b	10	quarters	13
c	4	thirds	7
d	7	fifths	10
e	2	tenths	4
f	5	sixths	8

2 Copy and complete the fraction sequences.

a $\frac{1}{4}, \frac{3}{4}, 1\frac{1}{4}, 1\frac{3}{4},$ ____ , ____ , ____ , ____ , ____

b $\frac{2}{6}, \frac{4}{6}, 1, 1\frac{2}{6},$ ____ , ____ , ____ , ____ , ____

c $\frac{1}{5}, \frac{3}{5}, 1, 1\frac{2}{5},$ ____ , ____ , ____ , ____ , ____

d $\frac{2}{10}, \frac{4}{10}, \frac{6}{10}, \frac{8}{10},$ ____ , ____ , ____ , ____ , ____

e ____ , ____ , ____ , $1, 1\frac{2}{8}, 1\frac{4}{8}, 1\frac{6}{8},$ ____ , ____

f ____ , ____ , ____ , $\frac{7}{10}, \frac{9}{10}, 1\frac{1}{10}, 1\frac{3}{10},$ ____ , ____

3 Write the rule for each sequence in Question 2.

1 Copy and complete the fraction sequences.

a ____ , ____ , ____ , $1\frac{2}{10}, 1\frac{5}{10}, 1\frac{8}{10},$ ____ , ____ , ____

b ____ , ____ , ____ , $2\frac{1}{4}, 3, 3\frac{3}{4},$ ____ , ____ , ____

c ____ , ____ , ____ , $1\frac{3}{5}, 2, 2\frac{2}{5},$ ____ , ____ , ____

d ____ , ____ , ____ , $4\frac{1}{2}, 6, 7\frac{1}{2},$ ____ , ____ , ____

e ____ , ____ , ____ , $1\frac{4}{6}, 2\frac{1}{6}, 2\frac{4}{6},$ ____ , ____ , ____

f ____ , ____ , ____ , $2, 2\frac{2}{7}, 2\frac{4}{7},$ ____ , ____ , ____

2 Write the rule for each sequence in Question 1.

3 Using the table on the right, write the fraction sequence using the given start number and rule. Write ten terms for each sequence.

	Start	Term-to-term rule
a	3	increase by $\frac{2}{5}$
b	10	increase by $\frac{3}{10}$
c	9	increase by $\frac{2}{7}$
d	5	decrease by $\frac{2}{6}$
e	8	decrease by $\frac{2}{3}$
f	12	decrease by $\frac{2}{10}$

39

Equivalent fractions

Identify, name and write equivalent fractions of a given fraction

Challenge 1

1 Use the fraction wall to identify all the fractions that are equivalent to a half.

Record your fractions like this:

$$\frac{1}{2} = \underline{\quad} = \underline{\quad} = \underline{\quad} = \underline{\quad}$$

2 Explain how you knew which fractions were equivalent to a half.

3 Write another two fractions that are equivalent to a half.

1									
$\frac{1}{2}$					$\frac{1}{2}$				
$\frac{1}{3}$			$\frac{1}{3}$			$\frac{1}{3}$			
$\frac{1}{4}$		$\frac{1}{4}$		$\frac{1}{4}$			$\frac{1}{4}$		
$\frac{1}{5}$		$\frac{1}{5}$		$\frac{1}{5}$		$\frac{1}{5}$		$\frac{1}{5}$	
$\frac{1}{6}$		$\frac{1}{6}$		$\frac{1}{6}$		$\frac{1}{6}$		$\frac{1}{6}$	$\frac{1}{6}$
$\frac{1}{8}$	$\frac{1}{8}$	$\frac{1}{8}$	$\frac{1}{8}$	$\frac{1}{8}$	$\frac{1}{8}$	$\frac{1}{8}$	$\frac{1}{8}$		
$\frac{1}{10}$	$\frac{1}{10}$	$\frac{1}{10}$	$\frac{1}{10}$	$\frac{1}{10}$	$\frac{1}{10}$	$\frac{1}{10}$	$\frac{1}{10}$	$\frac{1}{10}$	$\frac{1}{10}$

Challenge 2

1 Use the fraction wall to identify all the fractions that are equivalent to a quarter.

Record your fractions like this:

$$\frac{1}{4} = \underline{\quad} = \underline{\quad}$$

2 Explain how you knew which fractions were equivalent to a quarter.

3 Use the fraction wall to identify all the fractions that are equivalent to a third.

4 Choose another fraction and find equivalent fractions.

1											
$\frac{1}{3}$				$\frac{1}{3}$				$\frac{1}{3}$			
$\frac{1}{4}$			$\frac{1}{4}$			$\frac{1}{4}$			$\frac{1}{4}$		
$\frac{1}{5}$		$\frac{1}{5}$		$\frac{1}{5}$		$\frac{1}{5}$		$\frac{1}{5}$			
$\frac{1}{6}$		$\frac{1}{6}$		$\frac{1}{6}$		$\frac{1}{6}$		$\frac{1}{6}$		$\frac{1}{6}$	
$\frac{1}{8}$	$\frac{1}{8}$	$\frac{1}{8}$	$\frac{1}{8}$	$\frac{1}{8}$	$\frac{1}{8}$	$\frac{1}{8}$	$\frac{1}{8}$				
$\frac{1}{9}$	$\frac{1}{9}$	$\frac{1}{9}$	$\frac{1}{9}$	$\frac{1}{9}$	$\frac{1}{9}$	$\frac{1}{9}$	$\frac{1}{9}$	$\frac{1}{9}$			
$\frac{1}{10}$	$\frac{1}{10}$	$\frac{1}{10}$	$\frac{1}{10}$	$\frac{1}{10}$	$\frac{1}{10}$	$\frac{1}{10}$	$\frac{1}{10}$	$\frac{1}{10}$	$\frac{1}{10}$		
$\frac{1}{12}$	$\frac{1}{12}$	$\frac{1}{12}$	$\frac{1}{12}$	$\frac{1}{12}$	$\frac{1}{12}$	$\frac{1}{12}$	$\frac{1}{12}$	$\frac{1}{12}$	$\frac{1}{12}$	$\frac{1}{12}$	$\frac{1}{12}$

1 Explain why any fraction that is equal to a half has to have a denominator that is a multiple of two.

2 Copy the fractions below.

If they are equivalent to a half, tick them. If they are not equivalent to a half, put a cross next to them.

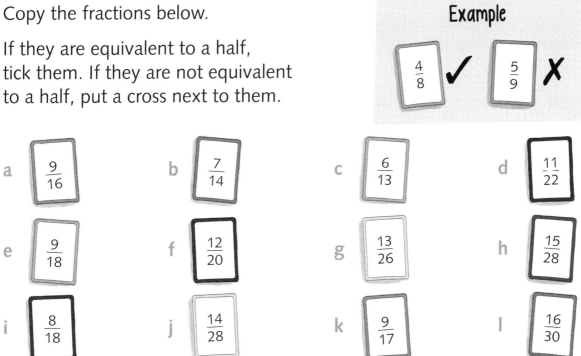

Example

$\frac{4}{8}$ ✓ $\frac{5}{9}$ ✗

a $\frac{9}{16}$ b $\frac{7}{14}$ c $\frac{6}{13}$ d $\frac{11}{22}$

e $\frac{9}{18}$ f $\frac{12}{20}$ g $\frac{13}{26}$ h $\frac{15}{28}$

i $\frac{8}{18}$ j $\frac{14}{28}$ k $\frac{9}{17}$ l $\frac{16}{30}$

3 Choose a fraction from Question 2 that is not equivalent to a half. Explain how you knew.

4 Work with a partner.

- Write six fractions that are equivalent to $\frac{3}{4}$ and six fractions that are not equivalent to $\frac{3}{4}$.
  Mix them up so they are not in two clear groups.

- Show the fractions to your partner.

- Ask them to tick the ones that are equivalent and put a cross next to the ones that are not equivalent.

Check their answers.

Ordering fractions

Compare and order fractions whose denominators are all multiples of the same numbers

Challenge 1

Order these fractions, smallest to largest, using the models.

a $\frac{1}{3}, \frac{1}{5}, \frac{1}{2}, \frac{1}{4}$

b $\frac{2}{5}, \frac{4}{6}, \frac{4}{5}, \frac{3}{6}$

c $\frac{3}{4}, \frac{3}{6}, \frac{2}{3}, \frac{2}{5}$

d $\frac{5}{8}, \frac{3}{10}, \frac{4}{6}, \frac{1}{2}$

e $\frac{6}{10}, \frac{1}{3}, \frac{5}{6}, \frac{3}{4}$

Challenge 2

1   Order these fractions, smallest to largest.

- Write out the multiples of the denominators to find the lowest common multiple (LCM).

- Change each fraction to its equivalent.

- Order the fractions.

Example

$\boxed{\frac{3}{4}}$ → 4, 8, <u>12</u>, 16, 20 $\frac{3}{4} = \frac{9}{12}$

$\boxed{\frac{1}{3}}$ → 3, 6, 9, <u>12</u>, 15 $\frac{1}{3} = \frac{4}{12}$

$\boxed{\frac{4}{6}}$ → 6, <u>12</u>, 18 $\frac{4}{6} = \frac{8}{12}$

$\frac{1}{3}, \frac{4}{6}, \frac{3}{4}$

a $\boxed{\frac{2}{5}}$ $\boxed{\frac{6}{10}}$ $\boxed{\frac{1}{2}}$ b $\boxed{\frac{2}{3}}$ $\boxed{\frac{5}{6}}$ $\boxed{\frac{1}{4}}$

c $\boxed{\frac{3}{4}}$ $\boxed{\frac{6}{10}}$ $\boxed{\frac{2}{5}}$ d $\boxed{\frac{2}{6}}$ $\boxed{\frac{2}{3}}$ $\boxed{\frac{5}{12}}$

e $\boxed{\frac{2}{7}}$ $\boxed{\frac{1}{2}}$ $\boxed{\frac{11}{14}}$ f $\boxed{\frac{4}{8}}$ $\boxed{\frac{2}{3}}$ $\boxed{\frac{1}{2}}$

2   What are your top tips for ordering fractions?

1

a Put the fractions above into groups that have multiples in common. Make four groups. Each fraction can go in more than one group.

b Which fraction is in the most groups? Why is this?

c Which fractions do not fit in any of the groups? For each fraction not in a group, write one other fraction it could be grouped with.

2 Order these fractions, smallest to largest.

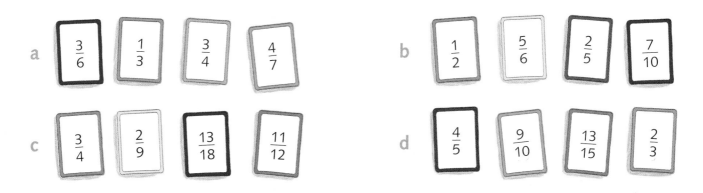

3 Jasmine has ordered these fractions like this:

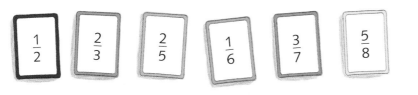

a How has she ordered them?

b Explain how she could have ordered them better.

c Now order the fractions in this way.

Translating shapes

Recognise where a shape will be after a translation on a 2-D grid

Challenge 1

In this grid, the shape has been translated three times.

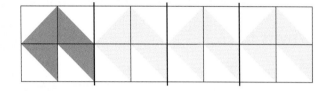

You will need:
- Resource 21: 2-D grids
- ruler
- coloured pencils

For each of these two shapes:

- copy the shape on to a 2 × 8 grid using Resource 21: 2-D grids

- translate the shape three times

- colour your design.

A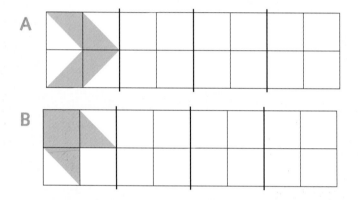

B

Challenge 2

1 In this grid, the shape has been translated three times. For each of the three shapes below:

- copy the shape on to a 4 × 4 grid using Resource 21: 2-D grids

- translate the shape three times into the smaller 2 × 2 grids

- colour your design.

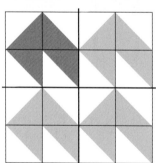

You will need:
- Resource 21: 2-D grids
- ruler
- coloured pencils

A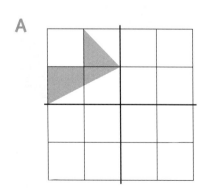

B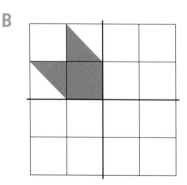

C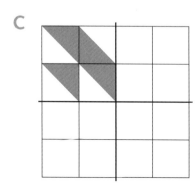

2 Copy this shape on to a 6 × 6 grid using Resource 21: 2-D grids.

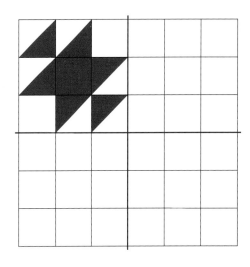

   a Translate the shape three times.

   b Colour your design.

3 Use a blank 6 × 6 grid on Resource 21: 2-D grids.

   a Draw your own shape in the top left set of 3 × 3 grids.

   b Translate your shape three times.

   c Colour your design.

Challenge 3

This Navajo blanket design is known as the 'Eye Dazzler'.

You will need:
- 1 cm triangular dot paper
- ruler
- coloured pencils

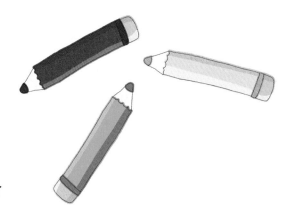

   a Copy the design below on to 1 cm triangular dot paper and colour it in.

   b Translate the design four times.

Tiling translations

Translate shapes to make a tiling pattern on a 2-D grid

 Challenge 1

Work with a partner.

Make these tiling patterns with your shapes.

A

B

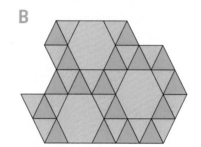

You will need:
- equilateral triangles tiles
- regular hexagons tiles

 Challenge 2

1 For each pattern below:

- copy it on to 1 cm square dot grid paper

- continue the pattern for four more large squares

- colour each section of the pattern so that the squares next to each other do not have the same colour.

You will need:
- 1 cm square dot grid paper
- coloured pencils
- ruler

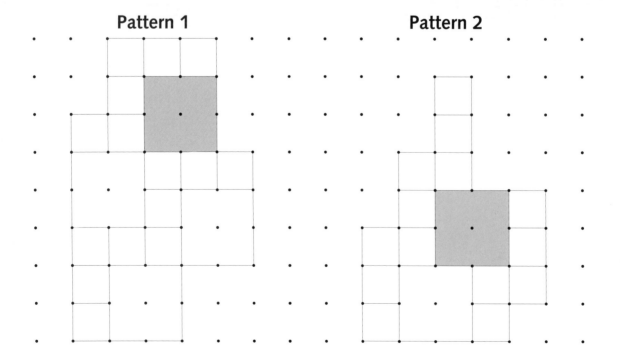

Pattern 1　　　　　　**Pattern 2**

2 Using two sizes of equilateral triangles, design your own translation pattern.

   a Copy it on to 1 cm triangular dot grid paper.

   b Colour your pattern.

Example

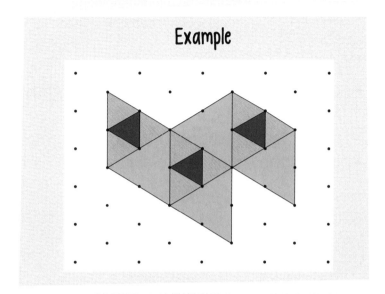

1 Work with a partner.

Use triangles, squares and hexagons to make these translation patterns.

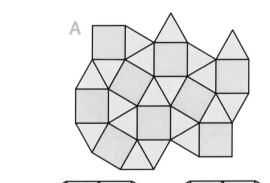

A

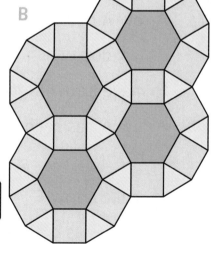

B

C

2 Use your regular polygons to make different tiling translations.

Translating polygons

Create 2-D shapes that will translate to form a tiling pattern

Challenge 1

For each shape below:

- copy it on to one of the square dot grids using Resource 22: 1 cm square dot grids
- translate each shape 1 dot to the right, then 1 dot up
- colour the shape in the overlap and name this shape.

You will need:
- Resource 22: 1 cm square dot grids
- ruler
- coloured pencils

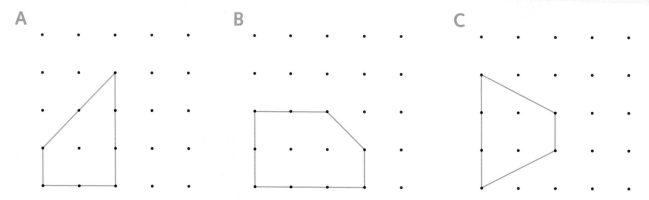

A   B   C

Challenge 2

1 Look at the circled vertices in the translation of the four arrows.

Copy and complete these sentences.

a   Arrow **A** has been translated

     dots

     to make arrow **B**.

b   Arrow **A** has been translated

     dots

     to make arrow **C**.

c   Arrow **D** has been translated

     dots

     to make arrow **B**.

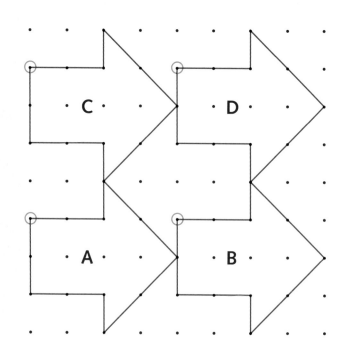

2 Use Resource 22: 1 cm square dot grids. For each hexagon:

- translate the circled vertex 2 dots up and complete the shape
- translate the circled vertex 2 dots down and complete the shape
- colour the 12 hexagons in the same colour.

Write what you notice about the white spaces between the coloured shapes.

You will need:
• Resource 22: 1 cm square dot grids
• ruler
• coloured pencil

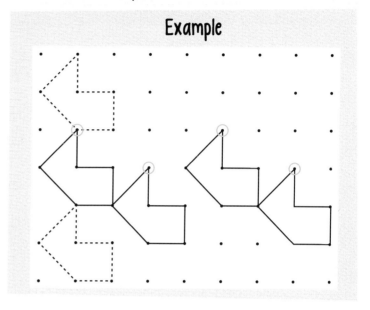

Example

Use Resource 22: 1 cm square dot grids. For each double-cross shape:
- translate the circled vertex 6 dots to the left and complete the shape
- translate the circled vertex 6 dots to the right and complete the shape
- colour the shapes in the same colour.

Write what you notice about the white spaces between the coloured shapes.

Example

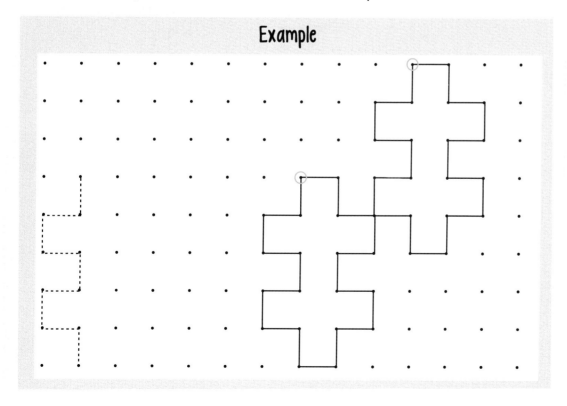

You will need:
• Resource 22: 1 cm square dot grids
• ruler
• coloured pencil

Translating with coordinates

Recognise where a shape will be after a translation on a coordinates grid

Challenge 1

Copy shape **A** on to Resource 23: 6 × 6 coordinate grids.

You will need:
- Resource 23: 6 × 6 coordinate grids
- ruler

a   Plot these points for shape **B**.

(4, 3) (5, 5) (6, 3)

b   Join the points in order.

c   Copy and complete the sentence for the translation:

Shape **A** has been translated _____ to the right then _____ up to make shape **B**.

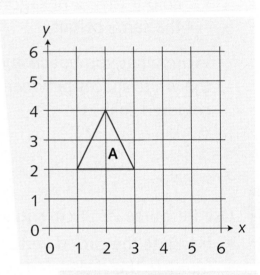

Challenge 2

1   The table shows the coordinates for the corresponding vertices for shapes **A**, **B** and **C**.

You will need:
- Resource 24: 9 × 9 coordinate grids
- ruler

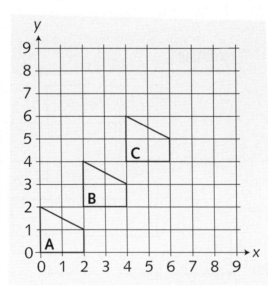

Shape	x-axis	y-axis
A	0	2
B	2	4
C	4	6
D		

a   Copy and complete the table. Work out and record the corresponding vertices for shape **D**.

b   Copy shapes **A**, **B** and **C** on to Resource 24: 9 × 9 coordinate grids.

c   Draw shape **D** on the grid.

2 Copy the shapes **A**, **B** and **C** on to Resource 24: 9 × 9 coordinate grids.

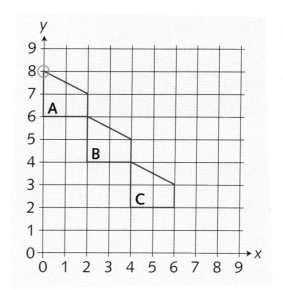

  a Copy and complete the table for the corresponding vertices for shapes **A**, **B** and **C**.

Shape	x-axis	y-axis
A	0	8
B	2	
C		
D		

  b Work out and record the corresponding vertex for shape **D**.

  c Draw shape **D** on the grid.

Copy shape **A** below on to Resource 24: 9 × 9 coordinate grids.

- Translate shape **A** by adding 2 units to the x-coordinate and adding 2 units to the y-coordinate, to create shape **B**.

- Translate shape **A** by adding 3 units to the x-coordinate and subtracting 1 from the y-coordinate, to create shape **C**.

- Repeat the first translation on shape **B** to create shape **D**.

- Repeat the second translation on shape **C** to create shape **E**.

- Shade the shapes using one colour for each translation.

You will need:
- Resource 24: 9 × 9 coordinate grids
- ruler
- coloured pencils

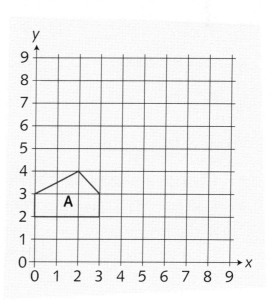

Adding mentally (2)

Add numbers mentally

34,875 + 400 = 35,275

1 Add these numbers mentally.

a 16,873 + 50   b 17,487 + 300   c 19,762 + 5,000

d 28,165 + 700   e 26,298 + 6,000   f 22,398 + 80

g 34,297 + 900   h 37,486 + 8,000   i 39,582 + 800

j 42,397 + 90   k 45,492 + 700   l 65,283 + 9,000

2 For each number, make three calculations by adding a multiple of 1,000, a multiple of 100 and a multiple of 10. Then work them out mentally.

a 26,143   b 32,871   c 35,065   d 40,297

e 46,816   f 53,522   g 57,392   h 63,824

Example

25,872 + 4,000 = 29,872

25,872 + 600 = 26,472

25,872 + 50 = 25,922

Challenge 2

1 Add these numbers mentally.

a 26,487 + 510   b 23,197 + 5,400   c 27,537 + 640

d 34,397 + 460   e 37,872 + 6,300   f 41,763 + 7,500

g 43,287 + 680   h 42,726 + 840   i 45,872 + 9,400

j 47,736 + 560   k 49,276 + 8,900   l 50,487 + 7,800

2 Work with a partner.

* Choose a 5-digit number together and write it down.
* Roll two dice. Use the digits and two 0s to make a 4-digit number. One of the 0s needs to be the 1s digit. So if you rolled a 3 and a 5, you could make 3,500, 5,300, 5,030 or 3,050.
* Both add the 4-digit number to the 5-digit number.
* Check you both get the same answer.

You will need:
* 2 × 1–6 dice

1 Add these numbers mentally.

a 54,872 + 670   b 57,387 + 7,900   c 58,877 + 540

d 53,384 + 860   e 63,983 + 8,200   f 68,598 + 6,600

g 74,498 + 730   h 77,498 + 9,700   i 84,873 + 7,500

2 Use mental methods to work out the missing numbers.

a 57,487 + ____ = 58,027   b 53,387 + ____ = 59,787

c 59,587 + ____ = 60,317   d 62,531 + ____ = 68,231

e 69,293 + ____ = 76,693   f 72,642 + ____ = 73,372

g 75,832 + ____ = 76,312   h 80,641 + ____ = 88,141

3 Work out the multiples of 1,000, 100 and 10 that have been added to the first number to equal the second number.

Example

| 52,634 | + 3,000 → | 55,634 | + 700 → | 56,334 | + 80 → | 56,414 |

a | 51,675 | + ____ → | | + ___ → | | + __ → | 55,995 |

b | 57,531 | + ____ → | | + ___ → | | + __ → | 63,961 |

c | 64,248 | + ____ → | | + ___ → | | + __ → | 72,448 |

d | 66,885 | + ____ → | | + ___ → | | + __ → | 74,275 |

e | 70,483 | + ____ → | | + ___ → | | + __ → | 76,393 |

f | 75,684 | + ____ → | | + ___ → | | + __ → | 81,234 |

Written addition (I)

- Add whole numbers using the formal written method
- Estimate and check the answer to a calculation

First estimate then calculate the answers to these calculations.

a   5,487 + 2,451

b   6,836 + 2,542

c   7,836 + 4,157

d   8,052 + 7,435

e   5,826 + 3,863

f   6,398 + 2,181

g   6,529 + 7,354

h   5,972 + 3,815

i   7,438 + 2,399

j   5,983 + 8,019

k   7,826 + 2,358

l   9,763 + 7,184

Example

$4{,}823 + 3{,}658 \rightarrow 4{,}800 + 3{,}700 = 8{,}500$

```
  4 8 2 3
+ 3 6 5 8
---------
  8 4 8 1
    1   1
```

Be sure to estimate and check the answers to your calculations.

1   First estimate then calculate the answers to these calculations.

a   16,746 + 37,192

b   27,871 + 21,593

c   37,615 + 43,137

d   28,716 + 30,557

e   18,673 + 45,291

f   48,761 + 21,299

g   53,867 + 42,563

h   47,827 + 39,091

i   36,846 + 52,518

j   47,736 + 29,931

k   56,836 + 38,097

l   62,762 + 24,818

Example

$46{,}825 + 57{,}504 \rightarrow 46{,}800 + 57{,}500 = 104{,}300$

```
    4 6 8 2 5
+   5 7 5 0 4
-------------
  1 0 4 3 2 9
        1 1
```

2   Add 47,835 to each of these numbers.

a    18,135

b   29,024

c   31,742

d   35,481

e   44,252

f    43,186

g    53,511

h    57,188

Example

$67{,}981 + 38{,}163 \rightarrow 68{,}000 + 38{,}000 = 106{,}000$

```
   6 7 9 8 1
+  3 8 1 6 3
  1 0 6 1 4 4
     1 1 1
```

1   First estimate then calculate the answers to these calculations.

a   17,836 + 26,819   b   29,376 + 25,295   c   37,762 + 11,489

d   42,074 + 38,557   e   47,173 + 35,288   f   41,764 + 55,679

g   53,062 + 39,489   h   50,637 + 46,784   i   49,386 + 38,905

j   58,274 + 46,486   k   76,387 + 23,845   l   86,244 + 49,387

2   Choose a 5-digit number.

Write five addition calculations with your number as the answer. No 0s allowed!

3   Add 67,516 to each of these numbers.

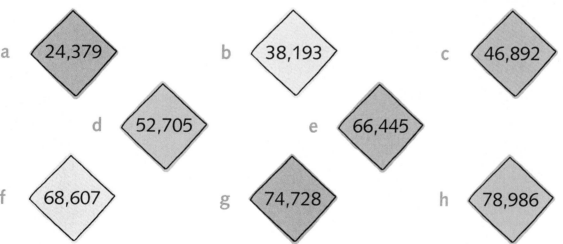

a   24,379   b   38,193   c   46,892

d   52,705   e   66,445

f   68,607   g   74,728   h   78,986

4   Three consecutive numbers have been added together to make these totals. What are the numbers?

a   53,199   b   86,235   c   57,306

d   91,275   e   81,792   f   67,002

Written addition (2)

- Add whole numbers using the formal written method
- Estimate and check the answer to a calculation

Example

$43,281 + 39,254 \rightarrow 43,300 + 39,300 = 82,600$

```
  4 3 2 8 1
+ 3 9 2 5 4
  8 2 5 3 5
      1   1
```

Challenge 1

1 First estimate then calculate the answers to these calculations.

a 14,682 + 12,145	b 15,735 + 11,524	c 18,528 + 11,357
d 24,726 + 13,192	e 19,376 + 25,413	f 23,386 + 25,702
g 21,628 + 27,254	h 36,387 + 13,911	i 28,517 + 35,241
j 32,292 + 35,462	k 41,365 + 32,827	l 26,386 + 46,251

2 Use the numbers on the balloons to write six addition calculations. First estimate then calculate the answers.

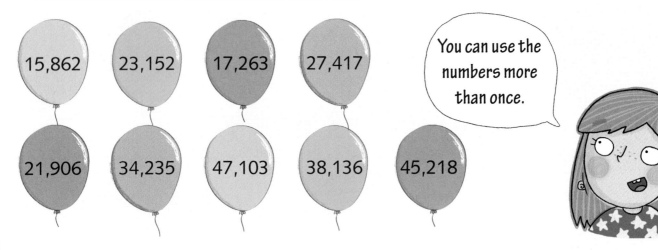

15,862   23,152   17,263   27,417

21,906   34,235   47,103   38,136   45,218

You can use the numbers more than once.

Challenge 2

1 First estimate then calculate the answers to these calculations.

a 37,486 + 36,951	b 29,487 + 31,066	c 34,382 + 39,753
d 42,398 + 31,825	e 28,175 + 42,355	f 40,673 + 22,677
g 39,271 + 35,349	h 50,439 + 46,793	i 46,276 + 47,477
j 41,836 + 44,474	k 56,318 + 39,284	l 68,286 + 27,992

2 Use the numbers on the balloons to write six addition calculations.
First estimate then calculate the answers.

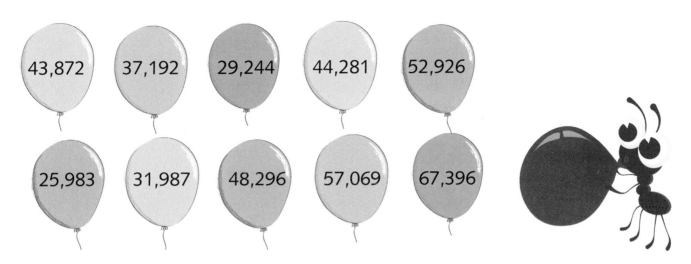

43,872 37,192 29,244 44,281 52,926

25,983 31,987 48,296 57,069 67,396

3 Two consecutive numbers have been added together to make these totals.
What are the numbers?

a 36,761   b 42,307   c 46,003   d 54,135   e 60,429

enge
3

1 First estimate then calculate the answers to these calculations.

a 47,371 + 36,849   b 35,483 + 37,827

c 41,398 + 49,823   d 45,262 + 45,958

e 48,475 + 44,635   f 56,483 + 37,759

g 32,476 + 59,755   h 45,222 + 47,888

i 54,836 + 63,575   j 61,845 + 62,486

k 72,265 + 51,967   l 77,482 + 60,769

Be sure to estimate and check the answers to your calculations.

2 Choose a 6-digit number.

Write five addition calculations with your number as the answer. No 0s allowed!

3 Write five 5-digit calculations for a partner to work out using the column method.

Checking calculations

- Add whole numbers using the formal written method
- Use rounding to check answers to calculations

Challenge 1

Work out these calculations using the formal written method. Then mentally answer the rounding calculation and use it to check your answer.

Example

```
  3 2 7 6 2
+ 2 3 6 1 5
  5 6 3 7 7
          1
```

Checking calculation:
32,800 + 23,600 = 56,400

a 14,763 + 12,825

   14,800 + 12,800

b 19,712 + 15,634

   19,700 + 15,600

c 16,265 + 14,173

   16,300 + 14,200

d 21,732 + 23,641

   21,700 + 23,600

e 25,387 + 24,152

   25,400 + 24,200

f 22,735 + 15,824

   22,700 + 15,800

g 31,365 + 12,274

   31,400 + 12,300

h 28,187 + 32,351

   28,200 + 32,400

i 34,696 + 21,802

   34,700 + 21,800

j 33,822 + 34,944

   33,800 + 34,900

k 42,581 + 25,637

   42,600 + 25,600

l 48,245 + 31,688

   48,200 + 31,700

Challenge 2

1 Work out these calculations using the formal written method. Then write the rounding calculation and use it to check your answer.

a 25,872 + 23,919

b 26,287 + 28,371

c 29,186 + 22,076

d 35,297 + 26,135

e 28,853 + 38,721

f 40,187 + 35,166

g 43,982 + 44,691

h 46,073 + 41,389

i 48,731 + 41,856

j 50,244 + 47,199

Example

```
  3 7 2 9 7
+ 4 3 5 6 1
  8 0 8 5 8
      1   1
```

Checking calculation:
37,300 + 43,600 = 80,900

2 Write two different calculations that could be checked
with these rounding calculations.

a (37,200) + (41,500)   b (18,900) + (28,300)

c (31,700) + (32,600)   d (44,100) + (27,800)

e (40,000) + (53,700)   f (51,200) + (38,600)

3 Work out how many numbers between 20,000
and 21,000 round up to the next multiple of 100.
How many round down?

1 Work out these calculations using the formal written method.
Then write the rounding calculation and use it to check your answer.

a   35,763 + 38,855   b   47,983 + 49,067

c   51,381 + 48,831   d   57,282 + 39,588

e   52,753 + 44,087   f   62,186 + 54,855

g   66,965 + 53,877   h   76,411 + 58,672

i   71,364 + 59,897   j   68,074 + 70,976

2 Why is it important to check the answer to a calculation?

Decimals as fractions

Read and write decimal numbers as fractions

 Challenge 1   Look at each grid. Write the decimal number and the fraction of the shaded area.

Example

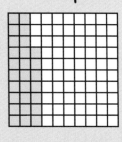

$$0.27 = \frac{27}{100}$$

a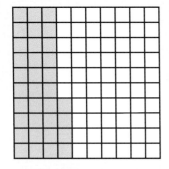

b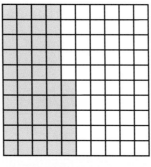

c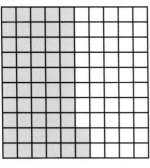

d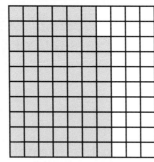

e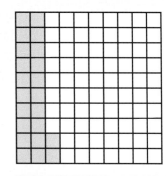

f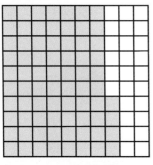

g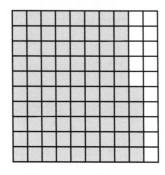

h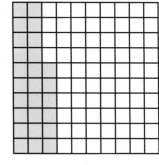

i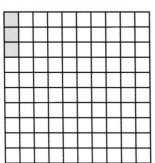

j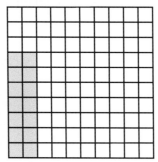

k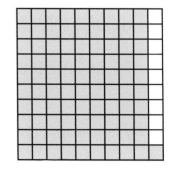

Challenge 2

1 Write each of these decimal numbers as a fraction.

a 0·6   b 0·52   c 0·11   d 0·9   e 0·83

f 0·04   g 0·27   h 0·1   i 0·01   j 0·99

2 Write each of these decimal numbers as a mixed number.

Example
$6·35 = 6\frac{35}{100}$

a 4·1   b 3·98   c 6·26   d 6·9   e 7·41

f 8·06   g 9·18   h 12·6   i 13·36   j 17·93

3 How are fractions and decimal numbers related?

Challenge 3

1 Write each of these decimal numbers as a mixed number and then as an improper fraction.

Example
$3·72 = 3\frac{72}{100} = \frac{372}{100}$

a 6·46   b 7·38   c 5·7   d 9·12   e 4·08

f 6·37   g 3·5   h 6·62   i 8·40   j 9·90

2 Are the decimal numbers in Questions 1 i and 1 j tenths or hundredths? Explain why.

Decimal rounding and complements

- Round decimals with 2 decimal places to the nearest whole number
- Add complements of 1

1   Use the number lines to round each decimal in the circles to the nearest whole number.

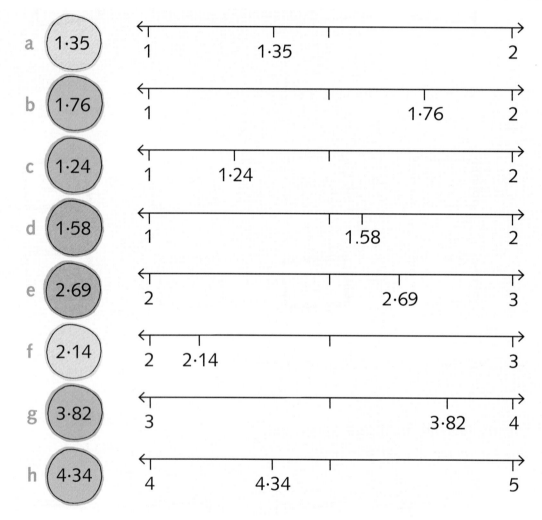

a (1·35)   1 ———————— 1·35 ———————— 2

b (1·76)   1 ———————— 1·76 ———— 2

c (1·24)   1 ——— 1·24 ———————— 2

d (1·58)   1 ———————— 1.58 ———— 2

e (2·69)   2 ———————— 2·69 ——— 3

f (2·14)   2 — 2·14 ———————— 3

g (3·82)   3 ———————— 3·82 —— 4

h (4·34)   4 ——— 4·34 ———————— 5

2   Round the decimals below without using number lines. Write the two whole numbers that each decimal number lies between and then circle the number it rounds to.

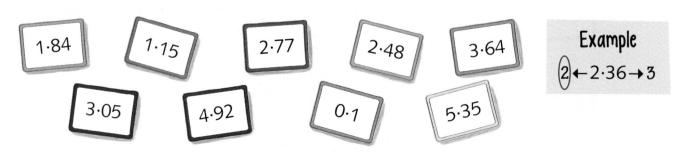

1·84   1·15   2·77   2·48   3·64

3·05   4·92   0·1   5·35

Example
②←2·36→3

1 Write the two whole numbers that each decimal number lies between and then circle the number it rounds to.

Example

$5 \leftarrow 5{\cdot}73 \rightarrow 6$

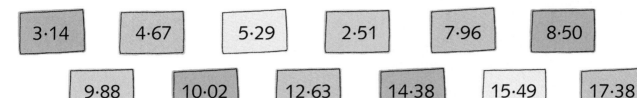

| 3·14 | 4·67 | 5·29 | 2·51 | 7·96 | 8·50 |

| 9·88 | 10·02 | 12·63 | 14·38 | 15·49 | 17·38 |

2 What needs to be added to the decimal numbers below to total 1? Write your answer as a calculation. You can use a number line to help your working out.

Example

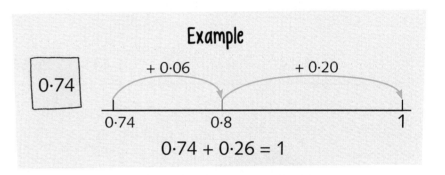

0·74

$+ 0{\cdot}06$ $+ 0{\cdot}20$

0·74   0·8   1

$0{\cdot}74 + 0{\cdot}26 = 1$

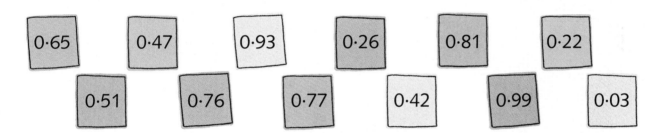

| 0·65 | 0·47 | 0·93 | 0·26 | 0·81 | 0·22 |

| 0·51 | 0·76 | 0·77 | 0·42 | 0·99 | 0·03 |

1 Write four decimal numbers with 2 places that can be rounded to each of the following numbers. Make sure you have two numbers that round up and two numbers that round down.

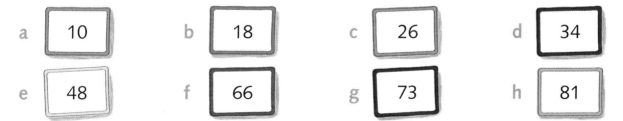

a 10   b 18   c 26   d 34

e 48   f 66   g 73   h 81

2 What needs to be added to these numbers to equal the next whole number? Write each answer as a calculation.

Example

16·36

$16{\cdot}36 + 0{\cdot}64 = 17$

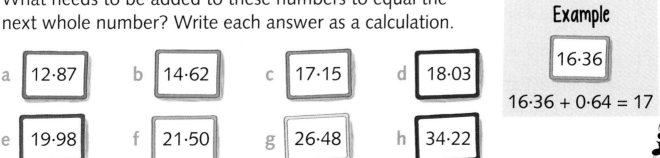

a 12·87   b 14·62   c 17·15   d 18·03

e 19·98   f 21·50   g 26·48   h 34·22

Rounding to 1 decimal place

Round decimals with 2 decimal places to 1 decimal place

Round all the red numbers on the number line to 1 decimal place.

1·26   1·39

1·14   1·32   1·43   1·55   1·68   1·86   1·79   1·95

1   1·1   1·2   1·3   1·4   1·5   1·6   1·7   1·8   1·9   2

1·63

1·6   1·7

Example

1·63 rounds to 1·6

Challenge 2

1 Use these instructions to draw a number line.

- Draw a line 20 cm long.

- Make a small interval every 2 cm.

- Write 3 at the beginning of the number line.

- Write 4 at the end of the number line.

- Mark your intervals 3·1, 3·2 … up to 3·9.

You will need:
- ruler

2 Write each of these decimals in the correct place on your number line.

a 3·02   b 3·12   c 3·19   d 3·35   e 3·43

f 3·51   g 3·59   h 3·65   i 3·77   j 3·96

3 Round each of the decimals in Question 2 to the nearest tenth.

Example
3·14 rounds to 3·1

4 Round each of these decimals to the nearest tenth.

a 4·28   b 5·03   c 5·65   d 6·49   e 6·98

f 7·27   g 8·33   h 9·82   i 9·15

1 Write all the decimals to 2 places that round to each of the numbers below.

a 3·5   b 5·6   c 6·9   d 7·1   e 8·0   f 9·3

g 10·8   h 12·2   i 14·7   j 15·4   k 6·5   l 13·3

2 Explain the rule for rounding numbers with 2 decimal places to the nearest tenth.

3 Play this game with a partner.

You will need:
• 2 × 1–6 dice

• Your target number is 0·3.

• Take turns to roll the dice. Use the two digits to make a decimal number to 2 places with 0 in the 1s column.

• Round your numbers to the nearest decimal to 1 place. The difference between your rounded number and 0·3 is your score.

• Do this ten times. The player with the lower score at the end is the winner.

Decimal sequences

Recognise and describe sequences involving decimals, and find the rule

Challenge 1

1 Copy each number sequence and write the next five numbers.

a 1·3, 1·5, 1·7,   ,   ,   ,   ,

b 3·2, 3·4, 3·6,   ,   ,   ,   ,

c 1·5, 2·0, 2·5,   ,   ,   ,   ,

d 0·4, 0·8, 1·2,   ,   ,   ,   ,

e 2·7, 2·9, 3·1,   ,   ,   ,   ,

f 5·9, 6·2, 6·5,   ,   ,   ,   ,

g 4·3, 4·6, 4·9,   ,   ,   ,   ,

h 7·5, 8·0, 8·5,   ,   ,   ,   ,

i 8·1, 8·5, 8·9,   ,   ,   ,   ,

j 6·8, 7·0, 7·2,   ,   ,   ,   ,

2 Copy each number sequence and write the next five numbers.

a 1·45, 1·46, 1·47,   ,   ,   ,   ,

b 0·32, 0·34, 0·36,   ,   ,   ,   ,

c 2·11, 2·13, 2·15,   ,   ,   ,   ,

d 2·50, 2·53, 2·56,   ,   ,   ,   ,

e 3·79, 3·81, 3·83,   ,   ,   ,   ,

f 4·01, 4·04, 4·07,   ,   ,   ,   ,

g 4·63, 4·66, 4·69,   ,   ,   ,   ,

h 6·25, 6·29, 6·33,   ,   ,   ,   ,

i 7·65, 7·70, 7·75,   ,   ,   ,   ,

j 8·14, 8·24, 8·34,   ,   ,   ,   ,

1 Copy each number sequence and write the missing terms.

a 2·1, 2·3, 2·5,   ,   ,   ,   ,

b 3·3, 3·6,   ,   , 4·5, 4·8   ,

c   ,   , 4·2, 4·4, 4·6,   ,   ,

d   ,   , 5·8, 6, 6·2,   ,   ,

e 0·1,   ,   ,   , 0·9, 1·1, 1·3,

f   , 2·6, 3·1,   ,   , 4·6, 5·1,

g   ,   ,   ,   , 4, 4·5, 5,

h 6, 6·4, 6·8,   ,   ,   ,   ,

2 Write the rule for each of the sequences in Question 1.

3 Copy each number sequence and write the missing terms.

a 0·48, 0·50, 0·52,   ,   ,   ,   ,

b   ,   ,   , 1·28, 1·30, 1·32,   ,

c   ,   ,   , 1·63, 1·66, 1·69,   ,

d   ,   ,   , 2·24, 2·28, 2·32,   ,

e 5·63,   ,   , 5·72, 5·75,   ,   ,

f   , 7·66, 7·76,   , 7·96,   ,   ,

g   ,   , 4·82, 5·82, 6·82,   ,   ,

h   ,   ,   ,   , 2·31, 2·36, 2·41,

4 Write the rule for each of the sequences in Question 3.

1 Write two different decimal number sequences for each rule.
Each sequence must include eight terms.

a The numbers increase by 0·04 each time.

b The numbers increase by 0·07 each time.

c The numbers decrease by 0·03 each time.

d The numbers decrease by 0·05 each time.

2 Write five different decimal number sequences. Include eight terms in
each sequence. Secretly write down the rule for each sequence and then
ask a partner to work out the rule for each one.

Converting masses

Convert between grams and kilograms

1 Write these masses in grams.

a $2\frac{1}{2}$ kg   b $4\frac{1}{10}$ kg   c $6\frac{1}{4}$ kg

d $3\frac{3}{10}$ kg   e $5\frac{7}{10}$ kg   f $7\frac{9}{10}$ kg

> **Example**
> $3\frac{1}{10}$ kg = 3,000 g + 100 g
> = 3,100 g

2 Write these masses in kilograms and grams.

a 6,260 g   b 9,530 g   c 6,060 g

d 9,500 g   e 6,200 g   f 9,030 g

> **Example**
> 2,040 g = 2,000 g + 40 g
> = 2 kg 40 g

3 Copy and complete.

a $3\frac{1}{2}$ kg = 3·   kg   b $3\frac{1}{4}$ kg = 3·   kg   c 3   kg = 3·75 kg

d 3   kg = 3·1 kg   e $3\frac{7}{10}$ kg = 3·   kg   f 3   kg = 3·9 kg

4 Write the mass of each kitten in grams.

> **Example**
> 2·25 kg = 2,000 g + 250 g
> = 2,250 g

a 2·5 kg

b 4·2 kg

c 3·25 kg

d 1·75 kg

e 3·6 kg

f 2·9 kg

1 Write these masses in kilograms and grams.

   a 4,350 g   b 3,920 g   c 5,180 g

   d 3,020 g   e 5,080 g   f 4,050 g

> **Example**
> 3,060 g = 3 kg 60 g

2 Write each of the masses in Question 1 in kilograms using decimals to 2 places.

> **Example**
> 3,060 g = 3·06 kg

3 Each of these scales shows the mass of 1 pack of 10 books.

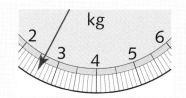

A   workbooks

B   textbooks

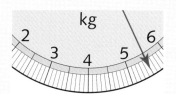

C   atlases

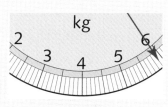

D   readers

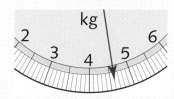

E dictionaries

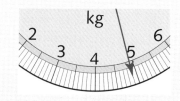

F history books

  a Write the mass of each pack of books:

     i   in kilograms to 1 decimal place

     ii in grams

  b For each pack, find the mass of 1 book:

     i   in kilograms

     ii in grams

  c Find the mass of 10 packs of each book in kilograms.

A primary school ordered 50 workbooks, 50 textbooks and 50 readers.
Find the total mass of their order.

Using metric and imperial units (1)

Know the imperial unit pounds (lb) and the rough metric equivalents in kg and g

Challenge 1

1 Copy and complete:

    a   lb ≈ 250 g

    b   lb ≈ 125 g

    c   lb ≈ 375 g

> **Rules**
> * There is a quick way to link imperial and metric masses. Use the fact that 1 lb is about 500 g.
> * ≈ means 'is approximately equal to'.

2 Write these approximate masses in grams.

    a $\frac{1}{2}$ lb   b $\frac{3}{4}$ lb   c $\frac{1}{4}$ lb   d 1 lb   e $1\frac{3}{4}$ lb

3 Using the symbol ≈ write the mass of each parcel in kilograms and in pounds.

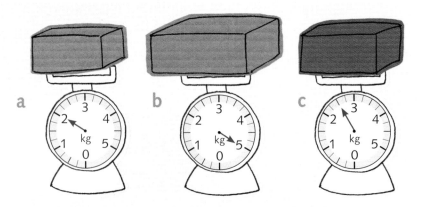

> **Example**
> $1\frac{1}{2}$ kg ≈ 3 lb

4 Using the symbol ≈ write the mass of each fish in pounds and in grams.

> **Example**
> $2\frac{1}{2}$ lb ≈ 1,000 g + 250 g
> ≈ 1,250 g

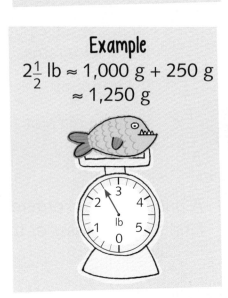

1 Using the approximate mass conversions on the right
   and the symbol ≈ write the mass that each scale
   shows in kilograms and in pounds.

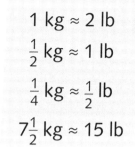

1 kg ≈ 2 lb

$\frac{1}{2}$ kg ≈ 1 lb

$\frac{1}{4}$ kg ≈ $\frac{1}{2}$ lb

$7\frac{1}{2}$ kg ≈ 15 lb

a 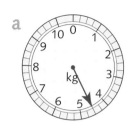   b 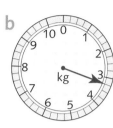   c 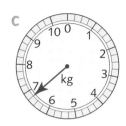   d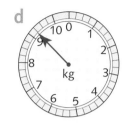

2 Write the approximate mass of the fruit in each bag in kilograms.

a 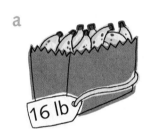   b 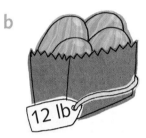   c    d

3 Use the pounds and grams scale on the right to convert
   these masses. Round your answers in a to the nearest
   10 g and in b to the nearest $\frac{1}{4}$ lb.

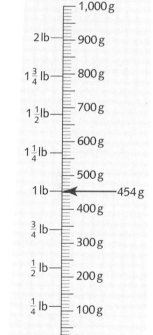

   a i $\frac{1}{2}$ lb   ii 1 lb   iii $1\frac{3}{4}$ lb   iv $1\frac{1}{4}$ lb

   b i 340 g   ii 910 g   iii 570 g   iv 120 g

4 Write **true** or **false** for each statement.
   Use the pounds and grams scale on the right to help you.

   a $\frac{1}{4}$ lb rounds up to 100 g   b $\frac{1}{2}$ lb is less than 200 g

   c 800 g ≈ $1\frac{3}{4}$ lb   d 2 lb > 1 kg

   e 700 g < $1\frac{1}{2}$ lb   f 1 lb ≈ 450 g

Find the mass of these fruits or vegetables to the nearest $\frac{1}{4}$ lb.

a    b    c 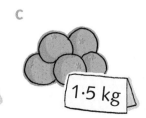   d

400 g   750 g   1·5 kg   1·25 kg

Mass problems

Use all four operations to solve problems involving mass

Challenge 1

1 Find the total mass of food in each bag.
   Write your answer in kilograms to 1 decimal place.

A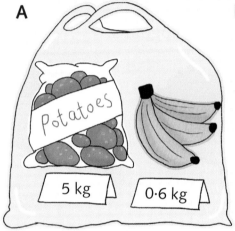

5 kg   0·6 kg

B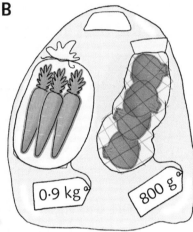

0·9 kg   800 g

C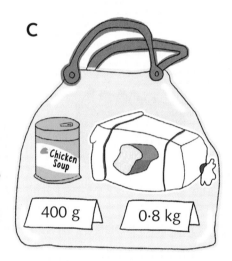

400 g   0·8 kg

2 How much heavier is shopping bag A:

   a than bag B?   b than bag C?

3 Find the total mass in kilograms of:

   a 3 loaves of bread   b 5 tins of soup

4 What is the approximate mass in grams of one banana?

Challenge 2

1 One medium-sized egg has a mass of 60 g.
   What is the mass in grams of 6 medium-sized eggs?

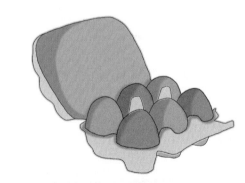

2 6 large eggs have a mass of about 400 g.
   About how many large eggs have a mass of 1 kg?

3 6 apples have a mass of 1·15 kg.
   Bill eats one of them.
   The remaining 5 apples have a mass of 0·97 kg.
   What was the mass of the apple that Bill ate?

4 Ben's mum made a dish for supper using 9 eggs and 12 fish fingers.

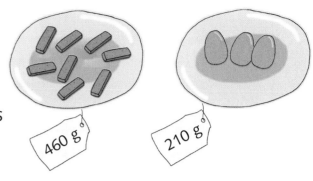

460 g

210 g

a Use the information in the pictures to work out the total mass in kilograms of the eggs and fish fingers she used.

b Once cooked, the dish weighed 1·24 kg. After supper, Ben's mum set aside $\frac{1}{4}$ of the dish for Ben's brother who would be home later. How many grams was this?

5 This display of tins of soup has a mass of 4·54 kg. The shopkeeper adds a fifth row of 5 cans of soup. What is the total mass of the tins of soup now in the display?

Two master and two apprentice sumo wrestlers need to cross a fast-flowing river.
The only transport available is a raft.
The maximum mass the raft will carry is 250 kg.

Hint
Draw a diagram to help you work out how the wrestlers get across the river.

Aki: 166 kg   **Beni:** 185 kg   **Chi:** 80 kg   **Do:** 91 kg

Find the least number of raft trips needed to get all four wrestlers across the river.

At Sara's Snack Bar

Use all four operations to solve problems involving mass and scaling

 Challenge 1

1 Work out the total mass of the snacks in each question. Write your answer in grams and in kilograms using decimals.

    a   1 baked potato and 1 apple

    b   1 sandwich and 1 banana

    c   1 cup of soup and 1 slice of quiche

2 Sara had an order for 10 cups of soup and 10 slices of quiche. What was the total mass of the order in kilograms?

Sara's Snack Bar	
Food mass per portion	
baked potato	250 g
slice of quiche	90 g
sandwich	175 g
cup of soup	140 g
banana	125 g
apple	150 g

 Challenge 2

1 Look at the Food mass per portion in the table in Challenge 1.
Copy and complete the table below for the number of sales at Sara's Snack Bar.

Food item	Number of sales		
	1 sale	10 sales	50 sales
baked potato	0·25 kg	2·5 kg	
slice of quiche	0·09 kg		
sandwich	0·175 kg		
cup of soup			
banana			
apple			

2 These bakery goods are displayed in Sara's shop window.

540 g
scones

350 g
doughnuts

cupcakes
320 g

For each plate of bakery goods, find the mass of:

a 1 item in grams   b 10 items in kilograms   c 100 items in kilograms

3 Mrs Hassan bought 3 scones, 3 doughnuts and 3 cupcakes.
Find the total mass of her purchases in kilograms.

4 Saturday is Sara's busiest day. She made 6·75 kg of scones.
How many scones did she make?

5 Sara's cat and its kitten together have a mass of 2·8 kg.
The cat's mass is 1,800 g more than the mass of the kitten.

a What is the mass of the cat?

b What is the mass of the kitten?

1 Sara's sons, Harry and George, take turns to stand
on a weighing machine with Bruce their dog.

• Harry and George have a mass of 83 kg.

• Harry and Bruce have a mass of 64·5 kg.

• George and Bruce have a mass of 59·5 kg.

Find the mass in kilograms of:

a Harry   b George   c Bruce

2 What is the total mass of Harry, George and Bruce?

Square and cube numbers

Recognise and use square numbers and cube numbers, and the notation for squared (^{2}) and cubed (^{3})

1   Some of the square numbers from 1 to 144 are missing in this number grid. Find the missing square numbers and write them in order, starting with the smallest number.

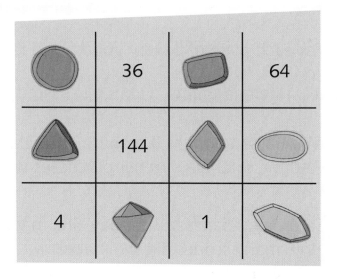

	36		64
	144		
4		1	

2   Write the calculation and answer for the first 12 square numbers.

Example
$4^2 = 4 \times 4 = 16$

1   Can you work out the first 10 cube numbers? Write the calculation for each cube number.

Example
$4^3 = 4 \times 4 \times 4 = 64$

a 1^3

b 2^3

c 3^3

d 4^3

e 5^3

f 6^3

g 7^3

h 8^3

i 9^3

j 10^3

2   Work with a partner.

  • Use centicubes to make cube numbers.
     See if you can make 1^3, 2^3, 3^3, 4^3 and 5^3.

You will need:
  • 125 centicubes

  • Check that the number of centicubes you have used is
     the same as your calculations in Question 1.

3   Write the answers to these calculations involving square numbers.
    Show your working out.

    a $6^2 + 5^2 + 4^2$ b $12^2 - 6^2 - 3^2$ c $9^2 + 7^2 + 5^2$

    d $11^2 + 10^2 + 12^2$ e $6^2 \times 2^2 \times 3^2$ f $9^2 \times 3^2$

llenge 3

Can you find pairs of calculations that are equivalent in value?
Work out the answer to each pair of calculations.
Which one in each pair was the easiest to work out?
Explain your reasons.

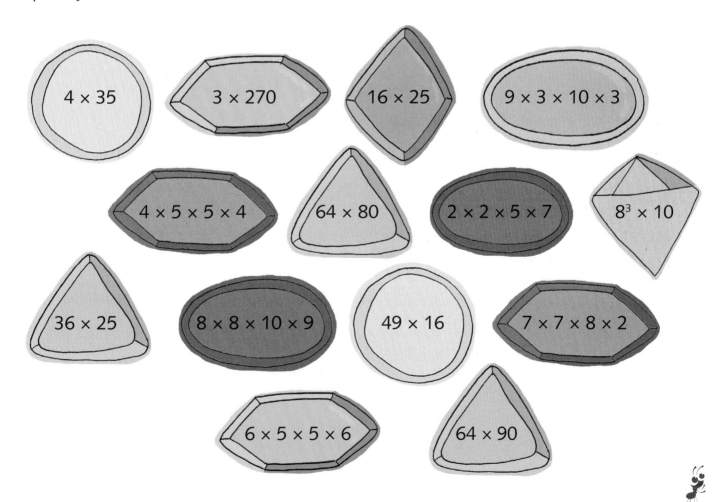

4 × 35

3 × 270

16 × 25

9 × 3 × 10 × 3

4 × 5 × 5 × 4

64 × 80

2 × 2 × 5 × 7

$8^3 \times 10$

36 × 25

8 × 8 × 10 × 9

49 × 16

7 × 7 × 8 × 2

6 × 5 × 5 × 6

64 × 90

Multiplying ThHTO × 0

- Use the formal written method to calculate ThHTO × O
- Estimate and check the answer to a calculation

1 Complete these multiplication facts.

a $4 \times 9 = \bigcirc$

b $\bigcirc \times 7 = 42$

c $8 \times 6 = \bigcirc$

d $9 \times \bigcirc = 72$

e $4 \times \bigcirc = 32$

f $7 \times \bigcirc = 56$

g $6 \times \bigcirc = 72$

h $\bigcirc \times 8 = 40$

i $\bigcirc \times 8 = 64$

j $9 \times \bigcirc = 54$

k $7 \times \bigcirc = 49$

l $6 \times \bigcirc = 54$

m $3 \times \bigcirc = 21$

n $8 \times \bigcirc = 40$

o $9 \times \bigcirc = 63$

p $\bigcirc \times 4 = 4$

q $7 \times \bigcirc = 0$

r $\bigcirc \times 6 = 36$

2 Write the answers to these calculations.

a 7×3
70×3
700×3

b 4×9
40×9
400×9

c 7×6
70×6
700×6

d 9×8
90×8
900×8

e 7×7
70×7
700×7

f 8×8
80×8
800×8

g 7×9
70×9
700×9

h 8×4
80×4
800×4

i 8×6
80×6
800×6

1 Estimate the answer to each calculation.

$3{,}273 \times 7 \rightarrow 3{,}000 \times 7 = 21{,}000$

a 3,546 × 3   b 5,732 × 4

c 5,648 × 5   d 6,273 × 9

e 3,986 × 6   f 8,888 × 8

g 7,676 × 7   h 6,869 × 6

```
      3 2 7 3
  ×  ₁ 5 ₂ 7
  ─────────────
    2 2 9 1 1
  ─────────────
```

2 Work out the answer to each calculation in Question 1 using the formal written method of multiplication.

Check your answer is close to your estimated answer.

 Write the missing digits in these calculations.

a
```
  □ 5 □ 7
  ×       □
  ─────────
  1 9 □ 8 1
```

b
```
  3 □ 2 □
  ×       9
  ─────────
  3 □ 6 □ 3
```

c
```
  □ 8 3 □
  ×       □
  ─────────
  1 9 3 2 8
```

d
```
  □ □ 7 □
  ×       8
  ─────────
  3 □ 0 □ 0
```

e
```
  6 7 □ 4
  ×       □
  ─────────
  2 □ 1 3 6
```

f
```
  3 □ 8 4 □
  ×         3
  ─────────
  1 0 9 3 5
```

Multiples and factors

Identify multiples and factors, including finding all factor pairs of a number, and common factors of two numbers

Challenge 1

1   The multiples are all jumbled up. Sort them into multiples of 6, 7, 8 and 9. Numbers can belong to more than one group.

| 6 | 18 | 54 | 42 | 30 | 21 | 56 |

| 49 | 64 | 32 | 72 | 81 | 63 | 36 | 45 |

2   In each bag, find the numbers that are factors of the number on the label.

> **Remember**
> A factor is a whole number that divides exactly into another whole number.

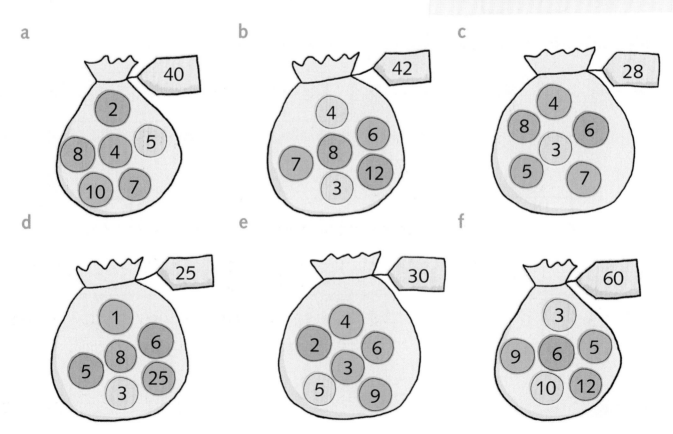

a   40: 2, 8, 4, 5, 10, 7

b   42: 4, 6, 8, 7, 12, 3

c   28: 4, 8, 6, 3, 5, 7

d   25: 1, 6, 8, 5, 25, 3

e   30: 4, 2, 6, 3, 5, 9

f   60: 3, 9, 6, 5, 10, 12

1 Write all of the factors of these pairs of numbers. Find and circle the common factors of both numbers.

Example

36, 40

36: ①,②, 3,④, 6, 9, 12, 18, 36

40: ①,②,④, 5, 8, 10, 20, 40

a 24, 30   b 36, 64   c 56, 80

d 45, 18   e 32, 48   f 60, 100

g 28, 42   h 20, 54   i 50, 35

j 34, 51   k 56, 24   l 72, 20

2 Write the first eight multiples for these pairs of numbers. Find and circle the common multiples of both numbers.

Example

2, 3

2: 2, 4,⑥ 8, 10, ⑫, 14, 16

3: 3,⑥ 9, ⑫, 15, 18, 21, 24

a 3, 4   b 4, 5   c 3, 6

d 4, 6   e 12, 16   f 15, 25

g 25, 50   h 8, 12   i 6, 9

1 Draw three different factor trees for each of these numbers.

a  24

b   48

c  64

d   81

e  36

f  72

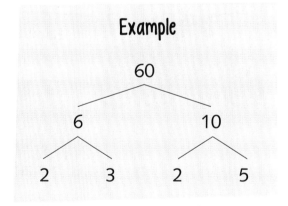

Example

60

6   10

2   3   2   5

2 What do you notice about the three factor trees for each number?

3 Make your own factor trees. Choose a number between 100 and 200. See how many different factors of each number you can find by drawing more than one factor tree.

Solving word problems (1)

Solve problems involving addition, subtraction, multiplication and division

Challenge 1

Work out the missing numbers.

a   43 × 10 =

b   ___ × 100 = 4,200

c   80 ÷ 2 =

d   364 ÷ 2 =

e   10 × ___ = 360

f   100 × ___ = 5,600

g   146 ÷ 2 =

h   ___ ÷ 2 = 156

i   ___ × 20 = 240

j   10 × ___ = 630

k   ___ ÷ 2 = 36

l   416 ÷ 2 =

Challenge 2

Answer these word problems.

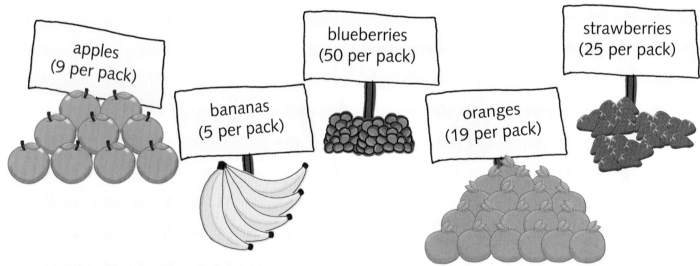

apples (9 per pack)

bananas (5 per pack)

blueberries (50 per pack)

oranges (19 per pack)

strawberries (25 per pack)

a   The supermarket has 466 packs of bananas to sell. How many bananas is this altogether?

b   The greengrocer sold 67 packs of oranges in a day. How many oranges is this altogether?

c   In one day, the supermarket sold 37 packs of strawberries and 85 packs of oranges. Which fruit did it sell more of?

d   There are 78 packs of blueberries on the shelf. How many blueberries altogether?

e John buys 3 dozen apples at a cost of 25p each. Mark buys 4 packs of apples for £7.20. What is the difference in their total cost?

f Single oranges cost 35p each. A pack of oranges costs £6. If I need 19 oranges, how much money do I save by buying the pack?

g The greengrocer made 68 packs of apples. How many apples did he have in total?

h The greengrocer has 3,273 strawberries. Can she package them all in packs without any being left over? Explain how you know.

i The greengrocer has 1,000 strawberries to package. Can he make 45 packs?

Challenge 3

Choose three of the fruits shown below.

watermelon   tomato   mango   lemon   grapes

1 Make up a word problem for each of your three fruits that involves one of the following operations:

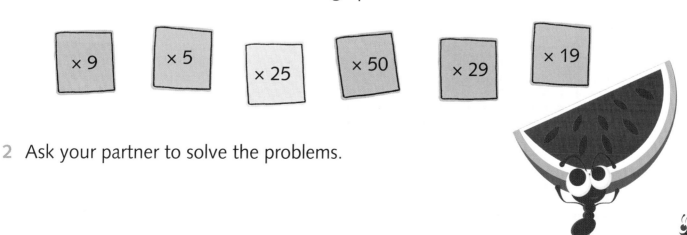

× 9   × 5   × 25   × 50   × 29   × 19

2 Ask your partner to solve the problems.

Prime numbers

- Know and use the vocabulary of prime numbers, prime factors and composite numbers
- Establish whether a number up to 100 is prime and recall prime numbers up to 19

Challenge 1

In each bag, find the numbers that are factors of the number on the star.

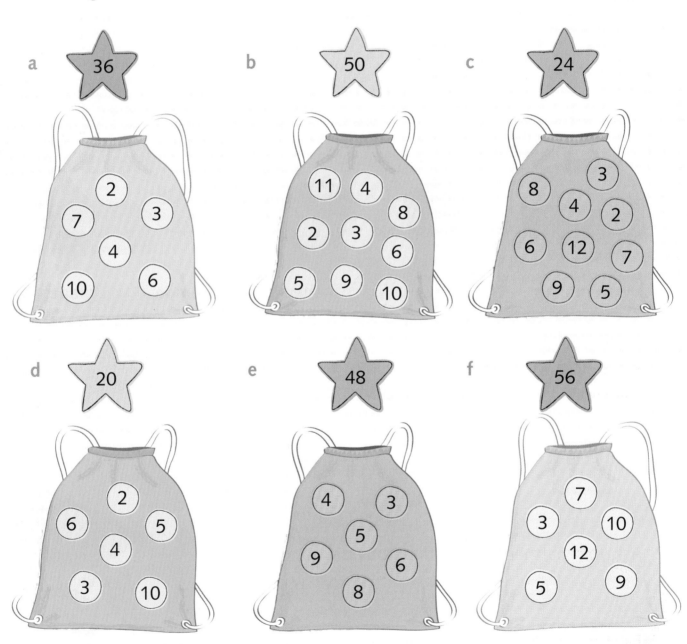

a 36

2 7 3 4 10 6

b 50

11 4 8 2 3 6 5 9 10

c 24

8 3 4 2 6 12 7 9 5

d 20

2 6 5 4 3 10

e 48

4 3 5 9 6 8

f 56

7 3 10 12 5 9

1 Sort the numbers below into two groups:

- prime numbers

- composite numbers

Next to each number, write its factors.

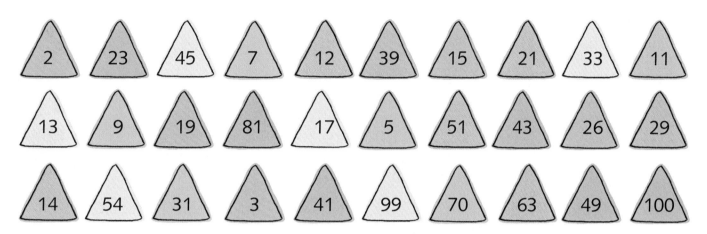

2 There are a total of 25 prime numbers from 1 to 100. Work with a partner to make a list of all 25. You've already found some in Question 1!

Which of these statements are correct? Explain how you know. Give examples to justify your explanations.

Division involving multiples of 10, 100 and 1,000

Divide whole numbers by 10, 100 and 1,000

 Challenge 1

1 a 60 ÷ 10	2 a 90 ÷ 10	3 a 360 ÷ 10
b 600 ÷ 100	b 900 ÷ 100	b 3,600 ÷ 100
c 6,000 ÷ 1,000	c 9,000 ÷ 1,000	c 36,000 ÷ 1,000
4 a 470 ÷ 10	5 a 63 000 ÷ 10	6 a 5,400 ÷ 10
b 4,700 ÷ 100	b 63,000 ÷ 100	b 5,400 ÷ 100
c 47,000 ÷ 1,000	c 63,000 ÷ 1,000	c 54,000 ÷ 1,000

Challenge 2

1 Work out the answers to these calculations.

a

21 ÷ 3

b

36 ÷ 4

c

63 ÷ 9

d

56 ÷ 8

e

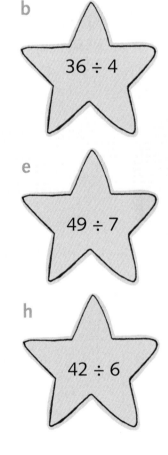

49 ÷ 7

f

72 ÷ 9

g

64 ÷ 8

h

42 ÷ 6

i

28 ÷ 7

2 These calculations are related to the calculations in Question 1.
Find the related facts. Group them together and work out the answers by using your knowledge of multiples of 10, 100 and 1,000.

a $210 \div 3$

b $4,900 \div 70$

c $6,300 \div 900$

d $630 \div 90$

e $49,000 \div 700$

f $360 \div 40$

g $72,000 \div 9$

h $560 \div 8$

i $36,000 \div 400$

j $56,000 \div 8,000$

k $6,300 \div 9$

l $2,100 \div 30$

m $490 \div 70$

n $560 \div 8$

o $7,200 \div 90$

p $4,200 \div 6$

q $640 \div 80$

r $6,400 \div 80$

s $28,000 \div 70$

t $42,000 \div 60$

u $2,800 \div 700$

1 Find the missing multiple of 10, 100 or 1,000.

a $2,300 \div$ ⭐ $= 23$

b ⭐ $\div 40 = 120$

c $6,400 \div$ ⭐ $= 80$

d $27,000 \div 30 =$ ⭐

e $4,800 \div$ ⭐ $= 240$

f ⭐ $\div 60 = 600$

g $9,000 =$ ⭐ $\div 6$

h ⭐ $\div 40 = 80$

i $24,000 \div$ ⭐ $= 6$

j $180 =$ ⭐ $\div$ ⭐

k $320 =$ ⭐ $\div$ ⭐

l ⭐ $\div 700 = 6$

1,000

100   *10*

2 Write three of your own division calculations involving multiples of 10, 100 and 1,000 that have these numbers as answers.

 9   35   63   14   27   54

Division ThHTO ÷ O using mental methods

Divide numbers mentally using known facts

1 These calculations are incomplete. Write the missing numbers.

a   54 ÷ 6 =

b   ÷ 4 = 8

c   4 ÷ 8 = 8

d   2   ÷   = 7

e   48 ÷   = 6

f   28 ÷ 7 =

g   6 ÷   = 9

h   6   ÷   = 12

i   ÷ 9 = 7

j   36 ÷   = 4

k   3   ÷ 4 = 8

l   7   ÷   = 11

m   ÷ 7 = 12

n   40 ÷ 5 =

o   108 ÷   = 12

p   ÷ 10 = 1

q   81 ÷   =

r   6   ÷   = 9

2 Work out these calculations.

a   8 ÷ 4
80 ÷ 4
800 ÷ 4

b   42 ÷ 7
420 ÷ 7
4,200 ÷ 7

c   24 ÷ 6
240 ÷ 6
2,400 ÷ 6

d   81 ÷ 9
810 ÷ 9
8,100 ÷ 9

e   49 ÷ 7
490 ÷ 7
4,900 ÷ 7

f   48 ÷ 8
480 ÷ 8
4,800 ÷ 8

g   54 ÷ 6
540 ÷ 6
5,400 ÷ 6

h   56 ÷ 8
5,600 ÷ 8
560 ÷ 8

i   44 ÷ 11
4,400 ÷ 11
440 ÷ 11

j   630 ÷ 9
63 ÷ 9
6,300 ÷ 9

k   4,900 ÷ 7
490 ÷ 7
49 ÷ 7

l   2,100 ÷ 3
21 ÷ 3
210 ÷ 3

Work out the answers to these calculations mentally.

a 324 ÷ 4	b 486 ÷ 6	c 5,614 ÷ 7	d 1,632 ÷ 4
e 6,030 ÷ 5	f 279 ÷ 3	g 288 ÷ 4	h 6,424 ÷ 8
i 4,228 ÷ 7	j 5,418 ÷ 6	k 497 ÷ 7	l 819 ÷ 9
m 4,836 ÷ 6	n 2,415 ÷ 3	o 3,672 ÷ 9	p 255 ÷ 5
q 219 ÷ 3	r 4,035 ÷ 5	s 6,390 ÷ 9	t 7,284 ÷ 8

1 Arrange each set of numbers to make a 3- or 4-digit number. Choose any number you like as a divisor so you are able to divide each one mentally. Try and create a calculation that you can work out mentally. Record your calculation and the answer.

Example
3,642 ÷ 6 = 607

Remember
The divisor is the number you divide by. So in the Example above, 6 is the divisor.

a   b

c   d

e   f   4   7   2   9

g   4   2   3   h   5   3   2   7

2 These numbers are the answers to some 4-digit divided by 1-digit division calculations that were worked out mentally. Write a division calculation for each answer.

Solving problems

Solve problems involving multiplication and division
including those involving factors and multiples

 Challenge 1

1   Each time the frog lands on a lily pad, the number on the
lily pad before is doubled. Write the missing numbers.

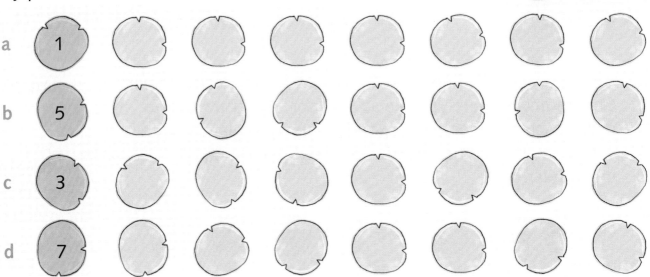

a   1

b   5

c   3

d   7

2   Halve each number.

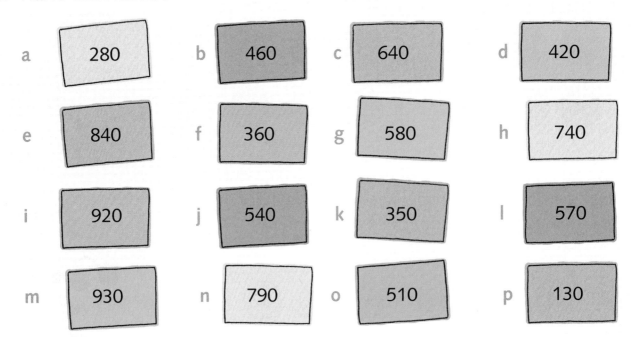

a   280   b   460   c   640   d   420

e   840   f   360   g   580   h   740

i   920   j   540   k   350   l   570

m   930   n   790   o   510   p   130

1 Use the doubling and halving strategy to find the answer to these calculations. Keep doubling and halving until you are able to work out the calculation mentally.

Example

$24 \times 36 = 48 \times 18$
$= 96 \times 9$
$= 864$

a 36×20 b 38×16 c 24×56

d 30×16 e 17×28 f 18×24

g 24×40 h 15×32 i 26×16

2 Choose two numbers from below to create your own doubling and halving calculations. Then find the answer. Write five of these calculations.

| 34 | 11 | 44 | 56 | 13 | 21 | 48 |

1 Use the doubling and halving strategy to find the calculation that is the odd one out in each set. Explain why the calculation is the odd one out.

a i 30×23 ii 15×46 iii 24×24 iv 17×21

b i 16×25 ii 28×15 iii 23×17 iv 36×13

c i 48×11 ii 12×22 iii 17×19 iv 15×16

d i 64×13 ii 26×35 iii 15×45 iv 17×28

2 Work out the answers to those calculations in Question 1 where it is possible to use the doubling and halving strategy.

Problems involving 12- and 24-hour clocks

Convert between units of time to solve problems

Challenge 1

1 Write the digital time to match these 12-hour times.

> **Example**
> 25 min to 10 is 9:35

a   15 min past 8

b   20 min past 7

c   25 min to 9

d   5 min to 10

e   10 min past 1

f   10 min to 4

2 Write the 12-hour times that these 24-hour digital clocks show. Remember to write p.m. after each 12-hour time.

> **Example**
> 19:00 is 7:00 p.m.

a   **19:45**

b   **14:40**

c   **21:06**

d   **23:30**

e   **16:24**

f   **18:51**

Challenge 2

1 The table shows the time each child took to swim 4 lengths of a swimming pool.

Alex	264 s
Paul	$4\frac{1}{2}$ min
Leah	3 min 50 s
Yasmin	4 min 8 s

a   Write the times for Paul, Leah and Yasmin in seconds.

b   How many seconds faster was Leah than:

   i   Alex?   ii   Paul?   iii   Yasmin?

c   Alex swam the first 2 lengths of the pool in 2 minutes and 16 seconds. How long, in minutes and seconds, did he take to swim the last 2 lengths of the pool?

2   The airport displays flight information on an Arrivals board.
    Write the scheduled arrival time for each flight as a 12-hour
    time. Remember to write a.m. or p.m. after the 12-hour time.

Arrivals board		
Scheduled arrival time	Arriving from	Remarks
09:50	Aberdeen	Landed 09:45
10:14	Oslo	Landed 10:40
11:32	Paris	Landed 11:32
12:45	Dubai	Expected 13:20
13:16	New York	Expected 12:56
13:38	Rome	Expected 14:15

Example
Aberdeen: 9:50 a.m.

3   Using the Arrivals board, answer these questions.

    a   Which flight arrived on time?

    b   Which flight landed 5 minutes early?

    c   By how many minutes was the flight from Oslo late?

    d   How many minutes ahead of the scheduled
        time is the flight from New York expected to land?

    e   By how many minutes is the flight from Dubai expected to be late in landing?

    f   What is the expected delay in minutes for the flight from Rome?

enge

1   Copy and complete the daily lunch
    break rota for four aircraft controllers:
    A, B, C and D. The order in which the
    controllers take the lunch breaks must
    differ each day, and each controller
    must have an equal chance of being
    first or last. Continue through the
    week until the rota repeats itself.

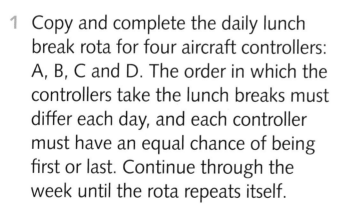

Day	Rota for lunch breaks			
	1st lunch	2nd lunch	3rd lunch	4th lunch
Monday	A			

2   The first lunch break starts at 11:45. If each lunch break is
    35 minutes long, work out the start time of the other lunch
    breaks, giving your answer in 24-hour clock time.

Timely calculations

Calculate durations of time to solve problems

1 For each customer at Greg's Garage:

a work out the time they take to wash their car and to vacuum its interior

b write the time using 24-hour notation when the tasks were finished.

- **Mr Adams**: arrived at 12:30, used car wash A then car vacuum B.

- **Mr Naseem**: arrived at 12:45, used car wash C then car vacuum C.

- **Mrs Duncan**: arrived at 13:10, used car wash B then car vacuum A.

Greg's Garage	
Car wash programme time	Car vacuum programme time
A 10 minutes	A 5 minutes
B 15 minutes	B 10 minutes
C 20 minutes	C 15 minutes

2 Mr Rossi finished at 14:20. He used car wash A then he used car vacuum C. At what time did he begin the car wash programme?

Hotel San Marco offers special rates to its guests when they book an activity for the times listed in the table.

Donna jots down the activity times from the hotel notice board and makes a list of what she would like to do on her holiday.

Activity	Start time	Finish time
Water skiing	15:15	17:10
Rock climbing	08:30	13:00
Canoeing	13:45	16:15
Tennis coaching	10:30	11:30
Mountain biking	10:00	13:30
Island trip by boat	14:00	17:45

a   Which activity takes the shortest time?

b   Which activity starts at 1:45 p.m.?

c   Which activity finishes at 10 past 5 in the afternoon?

d   Which activity takes $4\frac{1}{2}$ hours?

e   List two activities Donna can do on the same day. Work out how long each activity will last.

f   Donna takes the boat trip to the island. The return trip is delayed by 20 minutes as the boat has to wait for late passengers.

   i   At what time does Donna get back to the mainland?

   ii   How long did the whole boat trip take?

1   Donna is puzzled about the time. The hands on the clock tower clock show 25 minutes past 10 and the digital clock in the village square shows 10:18. A local resident tells her that one clock is always 4 minutes fast and the other is 3 minutes slow. What is the actual time?

2   On a 24-hour digital clock there are times when the minutes digits add up to the hours digit, for example 11:56 and 14:59. Which hours have the most of these times?

Time problems

Use all four operations to solve problems involving time

Challenge 1

Copy and complete.

a   2 min =   s   b   4 min =   s

c   2 h =   min   d   6 h =   min

e   2 days =   h   f   10 days =   h

g   2 weeks =   days   h   7 weeks =   days

i   2 years =   months   j   5 years =   months

Challenge 2

1   For how many months have a couple been married when they celebrate:

a   their Silver Wedding Anniversary?

b   their Ruby Wedding Anniversary?

c   their Golden Wedding Anniversary?

> **Hint**
> Silver Wedding: 25 years
> Ruby Wedding: 40 years
> Golden Wedding: 50 years

2   Anne Boleyn was the second wife of King Henry VIII. She was his queen for 1,000 days.

Work out how long she was Queen of England in years and days.

3   The *Charlotte Dundas*, the world's first boat to be powered by a steam engine, began service on the Forth and Clyde Canal in March 1803. A period of 9 years and 5 months later the *Comet*, the world's first passenger steamboat, began service on the River Clyde.

Write the month and the year when the *Comet* began service.

4 A cruise liner is on a round-the-world voyage.

a The cruise liner takes 51 days to sail from Southampton, via the Americas, to Sydney in Australia. How long is the cruise in weeks and days?

b The cruise liner then takes 61 days for the return voyage from Sydney, via Asian ports, to Southampton. How long is the return voyage in weeks and days?

c How many weeks does it take the cruise liner to complete its world voyage?

5 A company claims that its new longer life light bulb will last for 5 years. For how many days should the light bulb last?

6 There are 365 days in one year. What is the date that is exactly halfway through the year?

llenge 3

1 The first ancient Olympic Games were held in Olympia, Greece in 776 BC. The last ancient Olympic Games were held in AD 392. How many years is it:

a from 776 BC to the present year?

b from 776 BC to AD 392?

2 The ancient Olympic Games were held every 4 years. How many ancient Olympic Games were held between 776 BC and AD 392?

3 The first modern Olympic Games were held in Athens in 1896. How many years is it from the first ancient Olympic Games to the first modern Olympic Games?

4 The modern Olympic Games have been held every 4 years except for in 1916, 1940 and 1944. How many modern Olympic Games have there been from Athens in 1896 to London in 2012?

More time problems

Use all four operations to solve problems involving time, including scaling

1 Write how many days there are in:

a 5 weeks   b 7 weeks   c 10 weeks

2 Write how many months there are in:

a 3 years   b 6 years   c 9 years

3 Convert 10 years to:

a months   b weeks

1 Look at the map and the table of driving times from Perth.

Driving times from Perth to:	
Inverness	3 h 20 min
Aberdeen	2 h 45 min
Dundee	42 min
Stirling	1 h 8 min
Edinburgh	1 h 22 min
Glasgow	1 h 38 min
Dumfries	3 h 47 min

Jim is a lorry driver based in Perth. Calculate how long it took Jim to drive from Perth to each place in the table and then back to Perth.

a Inverness

b Aberdeen

c Dundee

d Stirling

e Edinburgh

f Glasgow

g Dumfries

2 In one week, Jim made 3 return trips to Aberdeen.
How long did he spend driving to and from Aberdeen?

3 Last winter, Jim was caught in a snowstorm as he drove back to Perth from Inverness.
The total time he spent on the journey to and from Inverness was 12 hours
10 minutes. How much time did the delays on the road add to his journey time?

4 In March, Jim made the same number of return journeys to both Edinburgh and
Glasgow. His log book shows 15 hours for these journeys. How many times did
he drive to both cities?

5 Find the time Jim recorded in his log book
for these return journeys to Stirling:

a 2 return journeys

b 4 return journeys

c 8 return journeys

Jim left Perth at 08:30 for Dumfries. Once he had made his delivery,
he took a break of 75 minutes for lunch and then began the drive
back to Perth. A road accident near Stirling added 25 minutes to
his journey time. At what time did he arrive back at the depot in Perth?

Maths facts

Problem solving

The seven steps to solving word problems

1 Read the problem carefully. **2** What do you have to find? **3** What facts are given?
4 Which of the facts do you need? **5** Make a plan.
6 Carry out your plan to obtain your answer. **7** Check your answer.

Number and place value

100,000	200,000	300,000	400,000	500,000	600,000	700,000	800,000	900,000
10,000	20,000	30,000	40,000	50,000	60,000	70,000	80,000	90,000
1,000	2,000	3,000	4,000	5,000	6,000	7,000	8,000	9,000
100	200	300	400	500	600	700	800	900
10	20	30	40	50	60	70	80	90
1	2	3	4	5	6	7	8	9
0·1	0·2	0·3	0·4	0·5	0·6	0·7	0·8	0·9
0·01	0·02	0·03	0·04	0·05	0·06	0·07	0·08	0·09

Positive and negative numbers

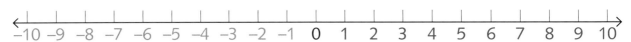

−10 −9 −8 −7 −6 −5 −4 −3 −2 −1 0 1 2 3 4 5 6 7 8 9 10

Roman numerals

I	V	X	L	C	D	M
1	5	10	50	100	500	1,000

Addition and subtraction

Example: 12,957 + 14,635

```
  1 2 9 5 7
+ 1 4 6 3 5
  2 7 5 9 2
    1     1
```

Example: 45,257 − 17,488

```
  3  14 11 14 17
  4̶ 5̶ 2̶ 5̶ 7̶
- 1 7 4 8 8
  2 7 7 6 9
```

```
  3  14 11 14 1
  4̶ 5̶ 2̶ 5̶ 7
- 1 7 4 8 8
  2 7 7 6 9
```

> You can also write the exchanged values like this.

Number facts

×	1	2	3	4	5	6	7	8	9	10	11	12
1	1	2	3	4	5	6	7	8	9	10	11	12
2	2	4	6	8	10	12	14	16	18	20	22	24
3	3	6	9	12	15	18	21	24	27	30	33	36
4	4	8	12	16	20	24	28	32	36	40	44	48
5	5	10	15	20	25	30	35	40	45	50	55	60
6	6	12	18	24	30	36	42	48	54	60	66	72
7	7	14	21	28	35	42	49	56	63	70	77	84
8	8	16	24	32	40	48	56	64	72	80	88	96
9	9	18	27	36	45	54	63	72	81	90	99	108
10	10	20	30	40	50	60	70	80	90	100	110	120
11	11	22	33	44	55	66	77	88	99	110	121	132
12	12	24	36	48	60	72	84	96	108	120	132	144

×	0·1	0·2	0·3	0·4	0·5	0·6	0·7	0·8	0·9	1	1·1	1·2
1	0·1	0·2	0·3	0·4	0·5	0·6	0·7	0·8	0·9	1	1·1	1·2
2	0·2	0·4	0·6	0·8	1	1·2	1·4	1·6	1·8	2	2·2	2·4
3	0·3	0·6	0·9	1·2	1·5	1·8	2·1	2·4	2·7	3	3·3	3·6
4	0·4	0·8	1·2	1·6	2	2·4	2·8	3·2	3·6	4	4·4	4·8
5	0·5	1	1·5	2	2·5	3	3·5	4	4·5	5	5·5	6
6	0·6	1·2	1·8	2·4	3	3·6	4·2	4·8	5·4	6	6·6	7·2
7	0·7	1·4	2·1	2·8	3·5	4·2	4·9	5·6	6·3	7	7·7	8·4
8	0·8	1·6	2·4	3·2	4	4·8	5·6	6·4	7·2	8	8·8	9·6
9	0·9	1·8	2·7	3·6	4·5	5·4	6·3	7·2	8·1	9	9·9	10·8
10	1	2	3	4	5	6	7	8	9	10	11	12
11	1·1	2·2	3·3	4·4	5·5	6·6	7·7	8·8	9·9	11	12·1	13·2
12	1·2	2·4	3·6	4·8	6	7·2	8·4	9·6	10·8	12	13·2	14·4

Written methods – short multiplication

Example: 378 × 4

Partitioning

$378 \times 4 = (300 \times 4) + (70 \times 4) + (8 \times 4)$
$= 1{,}200 + 280 + 32$
$= 1{,}512$

Grid method

×	300	70	8	
4	1,200	280	32	= 1,512

Expanded written method

```
    378
  ×   4
     32  (8 × 4)
    280  (70 × 4)
   1200  (300 × 4)
   1512
    1
```

Formal written method

```
    378          378
  ×   4      × 3 3 4
  1 5 1 2    1 5 1 2
    3 3
```

> You can also write the regrouped values like this.

Written methods – long multiplication

Example: 78 × 34

Partitioning

$78 \times 34 = (78 \times 30) + (78 \times 4)$
$= 2{,}340 + 312$
$= 2{,}652$

Grid method

×	70	8	
30	2,100	240	2,340
4	280	32	+ 312
			2,652

Expanded written method

```
       7 8
  ×    3 4
       3 2  (8 × 4)
     2 8 0  (70 × 4)
     2 4 0  (8 × 30)
   2 1 0 0  (70 × 30)
   2 6 5 2
       1
```

Formal written method

```
       7 8
  ×    3 4
   3 1³2   (78 × 4)
 2 3²4 0   (78 × 30)
 2 6 5 2
```

Written methods – short division

Example: 279 ÷ 6

Expanded written method	Whole number remainder	Formal written method

Fraction remainder | Decimal remainder

Expanded written method

```
    0 4 6  r 3
6) 2 7 9
  - 2 4 0
      3 9
  -   3 6
        3
```

Whole number remainder

```
    4 6 r 3
6) 2 ²7 ³9
```

Fraction remainder

```
    4 6 ½
6) 2 ²7 ³9
```

Decimal remainder

```
    4 6 · 5
6) 2 ²7 ³9 · ³0
```

Fractions, decimals and percentages

$\frac{1}{100} = 0{\cdot}01 = 1\%$

$\frac{2}{100} = \frac{1}{50} = 0{\cdot}02 = 2\%$

$\frac{4}{100} = \frac{1}{25} = 0{\cdot}04 = 4\%$

$\frac{5}{100} = \frac{1}{20} = 0{\cdot}05 = 5\%$

$\frac{10}{100} = \frac{1}{10} = 0{\cdot}1 = 10\%$

$\frac{20}{100} = \frac{1}{5} = 0{\cdot}2 = 20\%$

$\frac{25}{100} = \frac{1}{4} = 0{\cdot}25 = 25\%$

$\frac{40}{100} = \frac{2}{5} = 0{\cdot}4 = 40\%$

$\frac{50}{100} = \frac{1}{2} = 0{\cdot}5 = 50\%$

$\frac{75}{100} = \frac{3}{4} = 0{\cdot}75 = 75\%$

$\frac{80}{100} = \frac{4}{5} = 0{\cdot}8 = 80\%$

$\frac{100}{100} = \frac{10}{10} = 1 = 100\%$

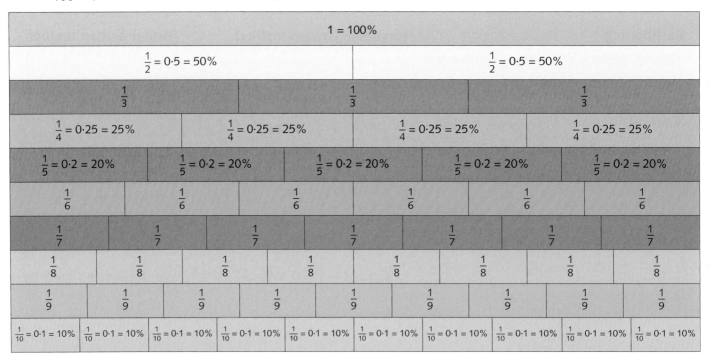

1 = 100%									
$\frac{1}{2} = 0{\cdot}5 = 50\%$					$\frac{1}{2} = 0{\cdot}5 = 50\%$				
$\frac{1}{3}$			$\frac{1}{3}$			$\frac{1}{3}$			
$\frac{1}{4} = 0{\cdot}25 = 25\%$		$\frac{1}{4} = 0{\cdot}25 = 25\%$		$\frac{1}{4} = 0{\cdot}25 = 25\%$		$\frac{1}{4} = 0{\cdot}25 = 25\%$			
$\frac{1}{5} = 0{\cdot}2 = 20\%$	$\frac{1}{5} = 0{\cdot}2 = 20\%$		$\frac{1}{5} = 0{\cdot}2 = 20\%$		$\frac{1}{5} = 0{\cdot}2 = 20\%$		$\frac{1}{5} = 0{\cdot}2 = 20\%$		
$\frac{1}{6}$	$\frac{1}{6}$		$\frac{1}{6}$	$\frac{1}{6}$		$\frac{1}{6}$	$\frac{1}{6}$		
$\frac{1}{7}$	$\frac{1}{7}$	$\frac{1}{7}$	$\frac{1}{7}$	$\frac{1}{7}$		$\frac{1}{7}$	$\frac{1}{7}$		
$\frac{1}{8}$	$\frac{1}{8}$	$\frac{1}{8}$	$\frac{1}{8}$	$\frac{1}{8}$	$\frac{1}{8}$	$\frac{1}{8}$	$\frac{1}{8}$		
$\frac{1}{9}$	$\frac{1}{9}$	$\frac{1}{9}$	$\frac{1}{9}$	$\frac{1}{9}$	$\frac{1}{9}$	$\frac{1}{9}$	$\frac{1}{9}$	$\frac{1}{9}$	
$\frac{1}{10}=0{\cdot}1=10\%$	$\frac{1}{10}=0{\cdot}1=10\%$	$\frac{1}{10}=0{\cdot}1=10\%$	$\frac{1}{10}=0{\cdot}1=10\%$	$\frac{1}{10}=0{\cdot}1=10\%$	$\frac{1}{10}=0{\cdot}1=10\%$	$\frac{1}{10}=0{\cdot}1=10\%$	$\frac{1}{10}=0{\cdot}1=10\%$	$\frac{1}{10}=0{\cdot}1=10\%$	$\frac{1}{10}=0{\cdot}1=10\%$

Add proper fractions

$\frac{2}{5} + \frac{4}{5} = \frac{6}{5}$

$= 1\frac{1}{5}$

Subtract proper fractions

$\frac{7}{8} - \frac{3}{8} = \frac{4}{8}$

$= \frac{1}{2}$

Multiply a proper fraction and a whole number

$\frac{2}{3} \times 4 = \frac{8}{3}$

$= 2\frac{2}{3}$

Multiply a mixed number and a whole number

$2\frac{3}{4} \times 3 = \frac{11}{4} \times 3$

$= \frac{33}{4}$

$= 8\frac{1}{4}$

Measurement

Length

1 km = 1,000 m = 100,000 cm
0·1 km = 100 m = 10,000 cm = 100,000 mm
0·01 km = 10 m = 1,000 cm = 10,000 mm
1 m = 100 cm = 1,000 mm
0·1 m = 10 cm = 100 mm
0·01 m = 1 cm = 10 mm
1 cm = 10 mm
0·1 cm = 1 mm

Metric units and imperial units – Length

1 km $\approx \frac{5}{8}$ miles (8 km $\approx$ 5 miles)
1 inch $\approx$ 2·5 cm

Perimeter and area

P = perimeter A = area
l = length   b = breadth

Perimeter of a rectangle
P = 2($l \times b$)

Perimeter of a square
P = 4 × l

Area of a rectangle
A = $l \times b$

Mass

1 t = 1,000 kg   1 kg = 1,000 g
0·1 kg = 100 g   0·01 kg = 10 g

Capacity

1 litre = 1,000 ml
0·1 l = 100 ml
0·01 l = 10 ml
1 cl = 10 ml

Time

1 millenium	= 1,000 years
1 century	= 100 years
1 decade	= 10 years
1 year	= 12 months
	= 365 days
	= 366 days (leap year)
1 week	= 7 days
1 day	= 24 hours
1 minute	= 60 seconds

24-hour time

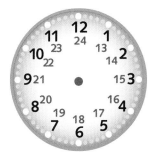

Properties of shape

2-D shapes

    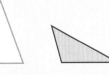 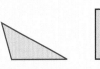

circle   semi-circle   right-angled
triangle   equilateral
triangle   isosceles
triangle   scalene
triangle   square   rectangle

103

2-D shapes (continued)

| rhombus | kite | parallelogram | trapezium | pentagon | hexagon | heptagon | octagon |

3-D shapes

cube   cuboid   cone   cylinder   sphere   hemi-sphere

triangular prism   triangular-based pyramid (tetrahedron)   square-based pyramid   octahedron   Dodecahedron

Angles

| Acute angle | Right angle | Obtuse angle | Straight line | Reflex angle | Whole turn |
| $< 90°$ | ($\frac{1}{4}$ turn) $= 90°$ | $> 90°$ and $< 180°$ | ($\frac{1}{2}$ turn) $= 180°$ | $> 180°$ and $< 360°$ | $= 360°$ |

Position and direction

Coordinates

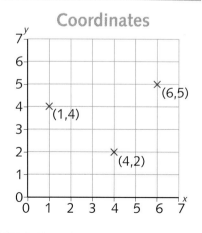

Translation

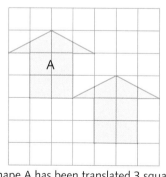

Shape A has been translated 3 squares to the right and 2 squares down.

Reflection

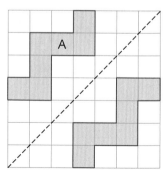

Shape A has been reflected along the diagonal line of symmetry.